THE LEADERSHIP GPS

GUIDING YOUR TEAM TO EXCELLENCE

ELIJAH M. JAMES, Ph. D.

Canadian Cataloguing in Publication Dada

James, Elijah M.

The Leadership Zone: Guiding Your Team to Excellence

ISBN 978-1-0689032-5-0

EJ Publishing

663 White Hills Run

Hammons Plains

Nova Scotia, Canada. B4B 1W7

To the countless leaders, mentors, and visionaries who have inspired and guided me along my journey.

To those who tirelessly strive to make a positive impact in their organizations and communities.

And to the future leaders who will shape the world with courage, compassion, and integrity.

This book is for you.

TABLE OF CONTENTS

PREFACE

———— ∞∞∞ ————

We occupy a world that is rapidly evolving—a world where change is the only constant. In such a world, effective leadership has never been more critical. The challenges we face today—technological advancements, global competition, economic fluctuations, and societal shifts—demand leaders who are not only adaptable but also visionary, compassionate, and resolute. **"The Leadership GPS: Guiding Your Team to Excellence"** is born out of a profound understanding of these dynamics and a commitment to empowering leaders to navigate their teams toward success.

This book is a culmination of years of experience, research, and insights gained from working with leaders across various industries and cultures. It offers a comprehensive guide to the principles and practices that define exceptional leadership. Whether you are a seasoned executive, a new manager, or an aspiring leader, the strategies and tools presented here will equip you to lead with confidence, clarity, and purpose.

In the pages that follow, you will discover the foundational elements of leadership, from self-awareness and emotional intelligence to effective communication and team-building. You will learn how to inspire and motivate your team, manage change, resolve conflicts, and foster a culture of innovation. Each chapter is designed to provide practical, actionable advice that you can apply immediately to your leadership journey.

What sets this book apart is its holistic approach to leadership development. We explore not only the skills and behaviours that make a great leader but also the mindset and values that underpin enduring success. Leadership is not a destination but a continuous journey of growth and improvement. **"The Leadership GPS"** serves as a trusted guide on this journey, helping you to chart a course through uncharted waters and reach new heights of excellence.

As you embark on this journey, I encourage you to reflect on your own leadership experiences, challenges, and aspirations. Use this book as a mirror to examine your strengths and areas for growth, and as a compass to navigate the complexities of leading a team in the modern world. Remember that leadership is both an art and a science, requiring a balance of intuition and analysis, empathy and decisiveness, vision and execution.

I am grateful to the many leaders who have shared their stories, insights, and wisdom with me over the years. Their experiences have enriched this book and inspired me to continue exploring the depths of leadership. I hope that **"The Leadership GPS"** will, in turn, inspire you to lead with excellence and make a meaningful impact on your team and organization.

Thank you for embarking on this journey with me. Together, let's set a course for leadership excellence and navigate toward a future of success and fulfillment.

With gratitude and best wishes,

Elijah M. James

INTRODUCTION

A. The Importance of Leadership in Today's Business World

In today's fast-paced and interconnected business environment, the role of leadership is more critical than ever. Leaders are the linchpins of organizational success, driving vision, fostering innovation, and steering their teams through periods of change and uncertainty. Effective leadership has become the cornerstone of sustainable growth and competitive advantage as businesses navigate the complexities of globalization, technological advancements, and shifting market dynamics.

Leadership is no longer just about making decisions from the top down. It is about inspiring and empowering others, creating a culture of trust and collaboration, and guiding teams to achieve their highest potential. The best leaders are those who understand the human element of business—who recognize that success is built not just on strategies and metrics, but on the strength, resilience, and creativity of their people.

In this evolving landscape, the ability to lead with clarity, compassion, and conviction is indispensable. Leaders must be adept at managing diverse teams, fostering inclusivity, and cultivating a shared sense of purpose. They must be agile, capable of adapting to rapid changes, and resilient in the face of challenges. Most importantly, they must possess a compass, a GPS—a guiding set of principles and values that direct their actions and decisions toward the greater good of their organization and its stakeholders.

B. How to Use This Book

"The Leadership GPS: Guiding Your Team to Excellence" is designed to be a comprehensive resource for leaders at all stages of their journey. Whether you are a seasoned executive seeking to refine your approach, a new manager stepping into a leadership role, or an aspiring leader looking to build a strong foundation, this book offers valuable insights and practical tools to enhance your leadership capabilities.

Structure and Content

The book is divided into six parts, each focusing on a critical aspect of leadership:

I The Foundation of Leadership: Explores the core principles and qualities that define effective leadership, including self-awareness, integrity, and emotional intelligence.

II Navigating the Leadership Landscape: Provides strategies for building strong teams, fostering communication, and motivating and empowering others.

III Leading Through Challenges: Offers guidance on managing change, resolving conflicts, and navigating crises with confidence and poise.

IV Strategic Leadership: Focuses on visionary leadership, innovation, and decision-making, providing tools to drive long-term success and organizational growth.

V Leadership Development: Covers mentorship, coaching, and training programs to help you develop future leaders and create a culture of continuous improvement.

VI A Look Toward the Future: Considers the importance of succession planning for the continuity of the organization, and looks at the nature of leadership in the future.

Practical Application

Each chapter includes real-world examples, case studies, and actionable advice that you can apply immediately in your leadership role. Reflective questions and exercises are designed to help you internalize the concepts and tailor them to your unique context.

Continuous Learning

Leadership is an ongoing journey of growth and development. Use this book as a reference guide to revisit and refine your leadership practices over time. The appendices offer additional resources, recommended readings, and tools to further support your learning.

By using **"The Leadership GPS"** as your guide, you will gain a deeper understanding of what it means to lead with excellence. You will learn how to align your team with a shared vision, inspire and empower others, and navigate the complexities of the modern business world with confidence and grace. Most importantly, you will develop a leadership map—a set of enduring principles and practices that will guide you on your journey to becoming an exceptional leader.

Welcome to the journey of leadership excellence.

PART I

THE FOUNDATIONS
OF LEADERSHIP

CHAPTER 1

DEFINING LEADERSHIP

"An effective leader has the following characteristics: self-confidence, strong communication and management skills, creative and innovative thinking, perseverance, willingness to take risks, open to change, levelheaded and reactiveness in times of crisis." Tech Target

A. Introduction

Leadership is a term that resonates across all spheres of life. Whether in business, politics, education, or community service, the presence of strong leadership is often the catalyst for progress and achievement. Yet, despite its ubiquity, leadership remains a concept that is frequently misunderstood and challenging to define. What does it mean to be a leader? How does one become an effective leader? In this chapter, we will explore the essence of leadership, delineate the traits that constitute great leadership, and distinguish leadership from management. By the end of this chapter, you will have a clearer understanding of the foundational elements of leadership and how they apply in various contexts.

B. What Makes a Great Leader

Great leadership transcends titles and positions. It is characterized by a set of intrinsic qualities and behaviours that inspire, motivate, and guide others toward achieving common goals. Some of the key traits that define a great leader include:

Vision

Great leaders possess a clear and compelling vision of the future. They can articulate this vision in a way that resonates with others, providing direction and purpose.

Integrity

Integrity is the cornerstone of trust. Leaders who consistently demonstrate honesty, transparency, and ethical behaviour earn the respect and loyalty of their followers.

Empathy

Understanding and connecting with the emotions and perspectives of others is crucial for building strong relationships and fostering a supportive environment.

Decisiveness

Effective leaders are able to make timely and well-informed decisions, even in the face of uncertainty. They take responsibility for their choices and are willing to adapt when necessary.

Inspiration

Great leaders inspire action. They ignite passion and enthusiasm in their teams, encouraging them to exceed their own expectations and achieve extraordinary results.

Resilience

The ability to bounce back from setbacks and maintain focus and determination in the face of challenges is a hallmark of strong leadership.

Communication

Clear and effective communication is essential for conveying vision, expectations, and feedback. Great leaders listen actively and foster open dialogue.

Adaptability

In a rapidly changing world, the ability to adapt and stay agile is vital. Leaders must be open to new ideas and willing to pivot strategies as needed.

Case Study

Sarah Martinez, the CEO of InnovateTech, (imaginary) exemplifies the qualities of a true leader through her visionary approach, empathy, and commitment to continuous growth. Taking the helm of the struggling tech startup, Sarah quickly assessed the company's strengths and weaknesses, and then crafted a clear and compelling vision that inspired her team to innovate and think creatively. She prioritized building a strong, diverse team, fostering an inclusive culture where every voice was valued, and encouraging collaboration across departments. Known for her open-door policy, Sarah made it a point to listen to her employees' concerns, empowering them to take ownership of their projects. Under her leadership, InnovateTech not only turned around its financial fortunes but also became known as a leader in ethical AI development. Sarah's ability to balance strategic foresight with genuine care for her people transformed the company and set a new standard for leadership in the tech industry.

C. Leadership vs. Management

While leadership and management are often used interchangeably, they are distinct concepts that play complementary roles in achieving organizational success. Understanding the differences between them is key to developing a balanced and effective approach.

Focus and Objectives

Leadership: Primarily concerned with setting direction, inspiring people, and fostering an environment of innovation and growth. Leaders focus on vision, change, and the long-term perspective.

Management: Concentrates on executing plans, organizing resources, and maintaining stability. Managers focus on achieving short-term goals, efficiency, and consistency.

Approach and Style

Leadership: Often involves a more transformative and motivational approach. Leaders challenge the status quo, encourage creativity, and empower their teams.

Management: Typically involves a more transactional and administrative approach. Managers ensure that tasks are completed, processes are followed, and results are measured.

People and Processes

Leadership: Focuses on people, their development, and their engagement. Leaders build relationships, influence culture, and mentor individuals.

Management: Focuses on processes, systems, and structures. Managers allocate resources, monitor performance, and ensure operational efficiency.

Change and Stability

Leadership: Embraces change and drives transformation. Leaders are forward-thinking and proactive in navigating new challenges.

Management: Values stability and seeks to minimize risks. Managers are often more reactive, ensuring that current operations run smoothly.

D. Sayings About Leadership

This section contains what others have said about leadership and teams. Some of the sayings are insightful, some are humourous, but all contain food for thought. They are all intended to be impactful as they deepen and widen your perspective of leadership. So smile a bit and learn a lot as you read and contemplate these sayings.

"Coming together is a beginning. Keeping together is progress. Working together is success."- **Henry Ford**

"Alone, we can do so little; together, we can do so much." – **Helen Keller**

"It is amazing what you can accomplish if you do not care who gets the credit." – **Harry S. Truman**

"Individually, we are one drop. Together, we are an ocean." – **Ryunosuke Satoro**

"Great things in business are never done by one person; they're done by a team of people." – **Steve Jobs**

"The way to get good ideas is to get lots of ideas, and throw the bad ones away." – **Linus Pauling**

"Creativity is thinking up new things. Innovation is doing new things." – **Theodore Levitt**

"Diversity is not only about bringing different perspectives to the table but also about creating an environment where everyone feels encouraged to contribute their unique ideas." – **Linda Naiman**

"Creativity is intelligence having fun." – **Albert Einstein**

"The role of a creative leader is not to have all the ideas; it's to create a culture where everyone can have ideas and feel that they're valued." – **Ken Robinson**

"The only way to achieve the impossible is to believe it is possible." – **Charles Kingsleigh (Lewis Carroll)**

"Success is stumbling from failure to failure with no loss of enthusiasm." – **Winston S. Churchill**

"Believe you can and you're halfway there." – **Theodore Roosevelt**

"The only person you are destined to become is the person you decide to be." – **Ralph Waldo Emerson**

"It always seems impossible until it's done." – **Nelson Mandela**

"No one can whistle a symphony. It takes a whole orchestra to play it." – **Halford Luccock**

"It takes two flints to make a fire." – **Louisa May Alcott**

"No man is an island, entirely of itself; every man is a piece of the continent." – **John Donne**

"If work isn't fun, you're not playing on the right team." – **Frank Sonnenberg**

"None of us is as smart as all of us." – **Ken Blanchard**

"If you can laugh together, you can work together." – **Robert Orben**

"A good team needs three things: the right people, the right spirit, and a couple inside jokes." – **Unknown**

"Work is the greatest thing in the world, so we should always save some of it for tomorrow." **– Don Herold**

"Teamwork means never having to take all the blame yourself." **– Stephen Hawking**

"Diamonds are nothing more than chunks of coal that stuck to their jobs." **– Malcolm Forbes**

"The best leaders are those the people hardly know exist." **- Lao Tzu,** *Tao Te Ching*.

"He who has learned how to obey will know how to command." **- Solon**

Source: https://www.teambonding.com/team-building-quotes/

E. Conclusion

Defining leadership is not about confining it to a single definition but rather understanding its multifaceted nature. Great leaders embody a blend of vision, integrity, empathy, and resilience, among other qualities. While leadership and management serve different functions, both are essential for the holistic success of any organization. As you delve deeper into the principles of leadership, remember that the journey to becoming an exceptional leader is ongoing. It requires continuous learning, self-reflection, and a commitment to personal and professional growth.

In the following chapters, we will explore these leadership qualities in greater detail, providing practical insights and strategies to help you develop and refine your leadership skills. By understanding and embracing the essence of leadership, you will be better equipped to guide your team to excellence and navigate the complexities of the modern business world.

CHAPTER 2

CORE LEADERSHIP PRINCIPLES

A. Introduction

At the heart of every effective leader lies a set of core principles that guide his/her actions, decisions, and interactions. These principles serve as the foundation upon which leadership is built, influencing not only the leader's behaviour but also the culture and success of his/her organization. In this chapter, we will explore the essential principles of integrity and ethics, vision and purpose, and empathy and emotional intelligence. Understanding and embodying these principles will enable you to lead with authenticity, inspire your team, and achieve sustained excellence.

B. Integrity and Ethics

Integrity and ethics are the bedrock of trust and credibility in leadership. Leaders who consistently demonstrate honesty, transparency, and ethical behaviour create an environment where people feel safe, valued, and respected. This trust is essential for fostering loyalty, collaboration, and a positive organizational culture.

Honesty

Honesty is more than just telling the truth; it's about being authentic and transparent in all dealings. Leaders who practice honesty encourage open communication and create a culture where issues are addressed directly and constructively. This approach helps prevent misunderstandings and builds a solid foundation of trust.

Transparency

Transparency involves being open about decision-making processes, organizational changes, and the rationale behind strategic choices. When leaders are transparent, they demystify their actions and reduce uncertainty, which can otherwise lead to anxiety and distrust among team members. Transparent leaders share both successes and setbacks, fostering a culture of continuous learning and improvement.

Ethical Decision-Making

Ethical decision-making requires a clear set of values and a commitment to doing what is right, even when it is difficult. Leaders face complex situations where the right choice isn't always obvious, and ethical considerations must guide these decisions. This includes considering the broader impact of actions on stakeholders, communities, and the environment. Leaders who prioritize ethics ensure their organizations operate responsibly and sustainably.

Consistency

Consistency in behaviour reinforces trust and reliability. Leaders who act consistently according to their stated values and principles set a standard for others to follow. This predictability in actions and decisions helps create a stable and trustworthy environment where team members know what to expect and feel secure in their roles.

Case Study

Consider the example of Paul Polman, former CEO of Unilever, who led the company with a strong commitment to sustainability and ethical business practices. Under his leadership, Unilever focused on reducing its environmental footprint and increasing its positive social impact, demonstrating how integrity and ethics can drive both business success and social good.

C. Vision and Purpose

A compelling vision and a clear sense of purpose are powerful motivators for both leaders and their teams. Vision provides direction, while purpose instills meaning and passion in the work being done.

Articulating the Vision

A vision statement should be clear, inspiring, and aspirational. It outlines the desired future state of the organization and serves as a rallying point for all members. Effective leaders are able to communicate their vision in a way that resonates with their team, creating a shared sense of destiny and a common goal to strive toward.

Aligning Goals

Aligning individual and team goals with the overarching vision ensures that everyone is working toward a common objective. This alignment enhances focus, coordination, and commitment, making it easier to prioritize tasks and allocate resources efficiently. Leaders must ensure that each team member understands how his/her role contributes to the larger vision, fostering a sense of ownership and accountability.

Purpose-Driven Leadership

Purpose goes beyond profit and productivity; it encompasses the values and impact the organization aims to have on its stakeholders and society. Leaders who embody this purpose inspire their teams to find meaning in their work. This sense of purpose can drive higher levels of engagement, motivation, and loyalty, as team members feel they are part of something larger than themselves.

Long-Term Perspective

Visionary leaders think beyond immediate challenges and opportunities. They anticipate future trends and prepare their organization to adapt and thrive in a constantly changing environment. This long-term perspective involves strategic planning, continuous innovation, and the willingness to take calculated risks to achieve sustainable growth.

Example

Elon Musk's vision for SpaceX to make space travel affordable and eventually colonize Mars exemplifies how a bold and clear vision can drive innovation and inspire a team. Despite numerous challenges and setbacks, Musk's unwavering commitment to this vision has propelled SpaceX to achieve groundbreaking milestones in space exploration.

D. Empathy and Emotional Intelligence

Empathy and emotional intelligence are crucial for building strong, effective relationships and fostering a positive organizational culture. Leaders who understand and connect with the emotions and perspectives of others can inspire loyalty, enhance collaboration, and improve overall team performance.

Understanding Others

Empathy involves actively listening to and understanding the feelings and viewpoints of others. This understanding fosters a sense of connection and trust, making team members feel valued and supported. Empathetic leaders are better equipped to address concerns, provide meaningful feedback, and create an inclusive environment where everyone feels heard.

Emotional Self-Awareness

Recognizing and managing one's own emotions is a key aspect of emotional intelligence. Leaders who are self-aware can navigate their own emotions and remain calm and effective under pressure. This self-awareness helps prevent emotional reactions from clouding judgment and allows leaders to respond to challenges with composure and clarity.

Effective Communication

Emotionally intelligent leaders communicate with sensitivity and clarity. They are adept at reading non-verbal cues and adjusting their communication style to meet the needs of their audience. This ability to connect on an emotional level enhances the effectiveness of their message and strengthens relationships within the team.

Conflict Resolution

Empathy and emotional intelligence are essential for resolving conflicts constructively. Leaders who can navigate emotional dynamics and understand underlying issues are better equipped to mediate and find mutually beneficial solutions. This approach not only resolves conflicts but also strengthens relationships and fosters a collaborative culture.

Case Study

Consider Satya Nadella, CEO of Microsoft, who is renowned for his empathetic leadership style. Under his leadership, Microsoft has undergone a significant cultural transformation, fostering greater collaboration, innovation, and inclusivity. Nadella's focus on empathy and emotional intelligence has helped rejuvenate Microsoft's corporate culture and drive its success.

E. Conclusion

Core leadership principles of integrity and ethics, vision and purpose, and empathy and emotional intelligence form the foundation of effective leadership. These principles not only guide leaders in their actions and decisions but also shape the culture and success of their organizations. By embodying these principles, leaders create an environment of trust, inspiration, and collaboration, enabling their teams to achieve excellence.

As you reflect on these core principles, consider how they manifest in your own leadership style and practice. Strive to integrate them into your daily interactions and decisions, and encourage your team to do the same. In the subsequent chapters, we will delve deeper into the practical applications of these principles, providing tools and strategies to help you lead with authenticity and purpose.

By understanding and embracing these core leadership principles, you will be better equipped to navigate the complexities of leadership, inspire your team, and drive your organization toward sustained success. Remember that leadership is a continuous journey of growth and improvement, and these principles will serve as your rudder, guiding you every step of the way.

CHAPTER 3

SELF-AWARENESS AND PERSONAL GROWTH

"Change and growth take place when a person has risked himself and dares to become involved with experimenting with his own life." – Herbert Otto

"It is always wise to keep in mind that neither success nor failure is ever final." –Roger Babson

A. Introduction

Self-awareness and personal growth are fundamental to effective leadership. Leaders who understand their strengths, weaknesses, and unique styles are better equipped to navigate challenges, inspire their teams, and drive success. Personal growth involves a commitment to continuous learning and adaptation, enabling leaders to evolve and thrive in an ever-changing landscape. This chapter explores the importance of self-awareness, the process of understanding your leadership style, and the value of continuous learning and adaptation.

B. Understanding Your Leadership Style

Every leader has a distinct leadership style shaped by his/her personality, experiences, and values. Understanding your leadership style is crucial for leveraging your strengths and addressing your weaknesses. It also helps in adapting your approach to different situations and individuals, enhancing your effectiveness as a leader. In the next section, we discuss various styles of leadership. This will enable you to identify your leadership style.

C. Various Styles of Leadership

Transformational Leadership

Description: Transformational leaders inspire and motivate their followers to achieve extraordinary outcomes and, in the process, help them develop their own leadership potential. These leaders are characterized by their ability to bring about significant change by articulating a compelling vision and encouraging innovation.

Key Characteristics:

- » Visionary and charismatic
- » Inspirational and motivational
- » Focused on personal and professional development of team members
- » Encourages creativity and new ideas
- » Leads by example

Example: Nelson Mandela is often cited as a transformational leader who inspired a nation through his vision of equality and reconciliation.

Transactional Leadership

Description: Transactional leaders focus on the exchange that occurs between leader and followers. This style is based on a system of rewards and penalties, where followers are rewarded for meeting specific goals and penalized for failing to meet them.

Key Characteristics:

» Task-oriented and directive
» Focuses on short-term goals
» Uses rewards and punishments to motivate
» Emphasizes performance and compliance
» Clearly defined roles and expectations

Example: Bill Gates during the early years of Microsoft used a transactional approach to drive performance and achieve company goals.

Servant Leadership

Description: Servant leaders prioritize the needs of their followers above their own. They focus on serving others and helping them achieve their potential. This style is characterized by empathy, listening, and a strong commitment to the personal growth of team members.

Key Characteristics:

» Focuses on the well-being and development of team members
» Practices empathy and active listening
» Builds a community within the organization
» Leads with humility and shares power
» Prioritizes service over self-interest

Example: Mahatma Gandhi exemplified servant leadership by dedicating his life to serving others and advocating for social justice.

Democratic (Participative) Leadership

Description: Democratic leaders involve their team members in decision-making processes. They value collaboration and seek input from their followers, ensuring that everyone's voice is heard before making a final decision.

Key Characteristics:

- » Encourages participation and collaboration
- » Values team input and feedback
- » Promotes a sense of ownership and accountability
- » Fosters open communication and transparency
- » Balances final decision-making authority with team input

Example: Google's management style often incorporates democratic leadership by encouraging employee input and fostering a culture of innovation.

Autocratic (Authoritarian) Leadership

Description: Autocratic leaders make decisions independently with little or no input from others. This style is characterized by a high degree of control and a focus on efficiency and results.

Key Characteristics:

- » Centralized decision-making
- » High degree of control and oversight
- » Clear directives and expectations
- » Limited team input
- » Emphasizes discipline and adherence to rules

Example: Steve Jobs was known for his autocratic leadership style at Apple, driving innovation and ensuring high standards.

Laissez-Faire (Delegative) Leadership

Description: Laissez-faire leaders provide minimal direction and allow their team members to make decisions. This style works well with highly skilled and self-motivated teams who require little supervision.

Key Characteristics:

- » Hands-off approach
- » High degree of autonomy for team members
- » Minimal oversight and intervention
- » Relies on team members' self-motivation and expertise
- » Provides support and resources as needed

Example: Warren Buffett employs a laissez-faire leadership style, trusting his managers to run their respective companies independently.

Situational Leadership

Description: Situational leaders adapt their style based on the needs of the team and the specific circumstances. They assess the situation and choose the most appropriate leadership approach, ranging from directive to supportive.

Key Characteristics:

- » Flexibility in leadership approach
- » Adapts to the needs of the team and situation
- » Balances directive and supportive behaviors
- » Focuses on team development and readiness
- » Tailors leadership style to individual team members

Example: A sports coach who adjusts his or her leadership style based on the team's performance and morale demonstrates situational leadership.

Transformational Leadership

Description: Transformational leaders inspire and motivate their followers to achieve extraordinary outcomes and, in the process, help them develop their own leadership potential. These leaders are characterized by their ability to bring about significant change by articulating a compelling vision and encouraging innovation.

Key Characteristics:

- » Visionary and charismatic
- » Inspirational and motivational
- » Focused on personal and professional development of team members
- » Encourages creativity and new ideas
- » Leads by example

Example: Nelson Mandela is often cited as a transformational leader who inspired a nation through his vision of equality and reconciliation.

Bureaucratic Leadership

Description: Bureaucratic leaders follow rules rigorously and ensure that their team adheres to processes and procedures. This style is effective in highly regulated environments where compliance is crucial.

Key Characteristics:

- » Strict adherence to rules and procedures
- » Focuses on consistency and efficiency
- » Emphasizes formal structures and hierarchies
- » Low flexibility and innovation
- » Clear roles and responsibilities

Example: Military leaders often employ bureaucratic leadership to ensure discipline and adherence to established protocols.

Charismatic Leadership

Description: Charismatic leaders use their charm and personality to inspire and influence their followers. They are often able to create a strong emotional connection with their team, leading to high levels of enthusiasm and commitment.

Key Characteristics:

- » Highly persuasive and inspiring
- » Strong emotional connection with followers
- » Uses charm and personality to influence
- » Visionary and forward-thinking
- » Relies on personal appeal

Example: Martin Luther King Jr. is an example of a charismatic leader who inspired millions with his vision and powerful oratory skills.

D. Identifying Your Style

As illustrated above, there are various leadership styles, such as transformational, transactional, democratic, autocratic, and servant leadership. Identifying your predominant style involves self-reflection and feedback from others. Tools like personality assessments, 360-degree feedback, and leadership development programs can provide valuable insights.

Strengths and Weaknesses

Understanding your strengths allows you to capitalize on what you do best, while recognizing your weaknesses provides an opportunity for growth. For instance, a transformational leader may excel at inspiring and motivating others but might need to work on operational details and consistency.

Adapting to Situations

Effective leaders are flexible and can adapt their style to meet the needs of different situations. For example, a democratic leader who values team input may need to take a more directive approach during a crisis to ensure swift decision-making and action.

Feedback and Reflection

Regularly seeking feedback from peers, mentors, and team members helps you gain a more accurate understanding of your leadership style. Reflection on your experiences and decisions further enhances self-awareness and informs your growth journey.

Case Study

Consider the example of Indra Nooyi, former CEO of PepsiCo, who combined aspects of transformational and servant leadership. Her focus on innovation and growth, coupled with a commitment to employee well-being, demonstrates the effectiveness of understanding and blending different leadership styles.

E. Continuous Learning and Adaptation

In the fast-paced and ever-evolving business environment, continuous learning and adaptation are essential for sustained leadership effectiveness. Leaders who prioritize personal and professional growth remain relevant, resilient, and capable of driving innovation.

Lifelong Learning

Embracing a mindset of lifelong learning involves seeking out new knowledge, skills, and experiences. This can be achieved through formal education, professional development programs, workshops, and self-study. Staying informed about industry trends, technological advancements, and best practices is crucial for maintaining a competitive edge.

Mentorship and Coaching

Engaging with mentors and coaches provides valuable guidance, support, and feedback. Mentorship relationships offer insights from experienced leaders, while coaching helps you set and achieve personal and professional goals. Both forms of support contribute to your ongoing development and growth.

Networking and Collaboration

Building a strong professional network allows you to learn from others, share experiences, and gain diverse perspectives. Collaboration with peers and industry experts fosters innovation and helps you stay adaptable in a rapidly changing environment.

Embracing Change

Adaptation involves being open to change and willing to pivot strategies when necessary. Leaders who embrace change and view it as an opportunity for growth are better equipped to navigate uncertainty and drive their organizations forward.

Example: Satya Nadella, CEO of Microsoft, exemplifies the importance of continuous learning and adaptation. Under his leadership, Microsoft has transformed its culture to emphasize learning, innovation, and customer-centricity, driving significant growth and success.

F. Conclusion

Self-awareness and personal growth are indispensable for effective leadership. Understanding your leadership style, leveraging your strengths, and addressing your weaknesses enhance your ability to lead with authenticity and impact. Continuous learning and adaptation ensure that you remain relevant, resilient, and capable of navigating the complexities of the modern business world.

As you progress in your leadership journey, remember that self-awareness is an ongoing process that requires regular reflection and feedback. Commit to lifelong learning, seek out mentorship and coaching, and embrace change as an opportunity for growth. By fostering self-awareness and personal growth, you will be better equipped to inspire your team, drive innovation, and achieve sustained excellence.

In the following chapters, we will delve deeper into the practical applications of these principles, providing tools and strategies to help you lead with confidence and purpose. Embrace the journey of self-awareness and personal growth, and let it guide you toward becoming the exceptional leader you aspire to be.

PART II

NAVIGATING
THE LEADERSHIP LANDSCAPE

CHAPTER 4

BUILDING A STRONG TEAM

"There's nothing greater in the world than when somebody on the team does something good, and everybody gathers around to pat him on the back."
– Billy Martin

"Teamwork is the ability to work together toward a common vision, the ability to direct individual accomplishments toward organizational objectives. It is the fuel that allows common people to attain uncommon results."
– Andrew Carnegie

A. Introduction

Building a strong team is one of the most critical responsibilities of a leader. A well-functioning team not only drives organizational success but also fosters a positive and collaborative work environment. This chapter delves into the essential aspects of team building, including recruitment and talent acquisition, creating a positive work culture, promoting diversity and inclusion, team development and training, and effective communication and collaboration. By focusing on these areas, leaders can assemble a team that is skilled, motivated, and aligned with the organization's values and goals.

B. Recruitment and Talent Acquisition

Recruitment and talent acquisition are foundational to building a strong team. Attracting and selecting the right candidates ensures that the organization has the necessary skills and competencies to achieve its objectives.

Defining Roles and Responsibilities

Clearly defining the roles and responsibilities for each position is crucial. This involves understanding the skills, experience, and attributes needed for success in the role. Job descriptions should be detailed and accurately reflect the requirements of the position. Studies have proved that results-oriented job descriptions are more effective the traditional duty-oriented job descriptions.

Attracting Talent

To attract top talent, organizations must showcase their strengths, including company culture, growth opportunities, and benefits. Utilizing various recruitment channels such as job boards, social media, and employee referrals can widen the talent pool. Additionally, employer branding--the process of getting employees on board with the mission, values, and vision of your organization--plays a significant role in attracting candidates who align with the company's values and mission.

Interview and Selection Process

A structured interview and selection process helps identify the best candidates. This process should include a combination of behavioural and technical interviews, assessments, and reference checks. Ensuring a fair and unbiased selection process is essential for attracting diverse talent.

Onboarding

Effective onboarding sets the tone for new hires. A comprehensive onboarding program should introduce new employees to the company's culture, values, and expectations. Providing the necessary resources and support during the initial phase helps new hires integrate smoothly and become productive members of the team.

Case Study

Google's rigorous and comprehensive recruitment process is a benchmark in talent acquisition. Their emphasis on cultural fit, diverse interview panels, and data-driven selection methods have helped them build a team of highly skilled and innovative professionals.

C. Creating a Positive Work Culture

A positive work culture is a key driver of employee engagement, satisfaction, and productivity. Leaders play a pivotal role in shaping and nurturing this culture.

Defining and Communicating Values

Clearly defined organizational values guide behaviour and decision-making. Leaders must communicate these values consistently and demonstrate them through their actions. This creates a shared sense of purpose and direction among team members.

Encouraging Open Communication

Open and transparent communication fosters trust and collaboration. Leaders should create an environment where team members feel comfortable sharing ideas, feedback, and concerns. Regular team meetings, one-on-one check-ins, and open-door policies can facilitate effective communication.

Recognition and Rewards

Recognizing and rewarding employees for their contributions reinforces positive behaviour and motivates continued excellence. This can include formal recognition programs, performance bonuses, and informal appreciation. Tailoring recognition to individual preferences can make it more meaningful and impactful.

Work-Life Balance

Promoting work-life balance is essential for employee well-being and long-term productivity. Leaders should encourage flexible work arrangements, provide resources for stress management, and support employees in balancing their professional and personal responsibilities.

Example: Zappos is renowned for its unique and positive work culture. Their focus on employee happiness, strong values, and customer-centric approach has not only driven business success but also created a highly engaged and loyal workforce.

D. Diversity and Inclusion

Diversity and inclusion (D&I) are vital for fostering innovation, creativity, and resilience within a team. An inclusive environment where diverse perspectives are valued leads to better decision-making and problem-solving.

Commitment to Diversity

Leaders must demonstrate a genuine commitment to diversity by setting clear goals, implementing D&I initiatives, and holding themselves accountable. This involves creating policies that promote equal opportunity and addressing any barriers to diversity.

Inclusive Leadership

Inclusive leaders actively seek out and value diverse perspectives. They create an environment where everyone feels respected, heard, and empowered to contribute. This involves challenging biases, promoting equity, and ensuring that diverse voices are included in decision-making processes.

Training and Development

Providing training on unconscious bias, cultural competency, and inclusive practices helps build awareness and skills among team members. Ongoing development opportunities ensure that D&I remains a priority and is embedded in the organization's culture.

Measuring and Monitoring

Regularly measuring and monitoring diversity metrics helps track progress and identify areas for improvement. This can include employee surveys, demographic data, and inclusion indices. Transparent reporting fosters accountability and drives continuous improvement.

Case Study

Salesforce's commitment to diversity and inclusion is exemplified through initiatives like their Office of Equality, employee resource groups, and transparent reporting on diversity metrics. These efforts have contributed to a more inclusive and innovative workplace.

E. Team Development and Training

Investing in team development and training is essential for maintaining a competitive edge and ensuring continuous improvement. Well-trained employees are more confident, efficient, and capable of contributing to the organization's success.

Skills Assessment and Development Plans

Regularly assessing the skills and competencies of team members helps identify areas for development. Personalized development plans that align with both organizational goals and individual career aspirations can drive growth and engagement.

Continuous Learning Opportunities

Providing ongoing learning opportunities through workshops, seminars, online courses, and mentoring programs helps employees stay current with industry trends and best practices. Encouraging a culture of continuous learning ensures that the team remains adaptable and innovative.

Leadership Development Programs

Developing future leaders within the organization is critical for long-term success. Leadership development programs that focus on enhancing leadership skills, strategic thinking, and decision-making capabilities can prepare high-potential employees for advanced roles.

Team-Building Activities

Regular team-building activities strengthen relationships, improve communication, and foster a sense of camaraderie. These activities can range from informal social gatherings to structured team-building exercises and retreats.

Example: IBM's emphasis on employee development includes extensive training programs, leadership academies, and continuous learning initiatives, which have been instrumental in maintaining their industry leadership.

F. Effective Communication and Collaboration

Effective communication and collaboration are the cornerstones of a high-performing team. Leaders must foster an environment where team members can communicate openly, share ideas, and work together effectively.

Clear Communication Channels

Establishing clear communication channels ensures that information flows smoothly within the team. This can include regular team meetings, project management tools, and collaboration platforms that facilitate seamless communication.

Active Listening

Leaders should practice active listening to understand the perspectives and concerns of team members. This involves giving full attention, asking clarifying questions, and providing thoughtful responses.

Conflict Resolution

Addressing conflicts promptly and constructively is essential for maintaining a harmonious team environment. Leaders should mediate conflicts with empathy and fairness, seeking solutions that satisfy all parties involved.

Collaborative Tools and Technologies

Utilizing collaborative tools and technologies can enhance team productivity and coordination. Project management software, video conferencing tools, and collaborative platforms like Slack or Microsoft Teams can streamline communication and project execution.

Example: Atlassian, known for its collaborative software products, embodies a culture of teamwork and communication. Their emphasis on transparent communication and use of collaborative tools has fostered a highly productive and innovative work environment.

G. Conclusion

Building a strong team is a multifaceted endeavour that involves strategic recruitment, fostering a positive work culture, promoting diversity and inclusion, investing in team development and training, and ensuring effective communication and collaboration. By focusing on these critical areas, leaders can create a team that is skilled, motivated, and aligned with the organization's values and goals.

Effective team building requires ongoing effort and commitment. Leaders must continuously evaluate and refine their approaches to recruitment, culture, inclusion, development, and communication to ensure they are meeting the evolving needs of their team and organization. By doing so, they can build a resilient and high-performing team capable of achieving sustained excellence.

As you continue your leadership journey, remember that the strength of your team is a reflection of your leadership. Invest in building a strong, diverse, and inclusive team, and you will unlock the full potential of your organization. In the next chapters, we will explore additional strategies and practices to enhance your leadership effectiveness and drive organizational success.

CHAPTER 5

EFFECTIVE COMMUNICATION

"The single biggest problem with communication is the illusion that it has taken place." –George Bernard Shaw

"To effectively communicate, we must realize that we are all different in the way we perceive the world and use this understanding as a guide to our communication with others." –Anthony Robbins

A. Introduction

E/ffective communication is the lifeblood of any successful organization. It is the foundation upon which relationships are built, strategies are executed, and goals are achieved. In leadership, the ability to communicate clearly and effectively is paramount. This chapter explores the essential elements of effective communication, including the principles of clarity, active listening, non-verbal communication, clear and concise messaging, feedback and constructive criticism, and the role of technology. By mastering these skills, leaders can foster a culture of openness, collaboration, and mutual respect within their teams.

B. Principles of Clarity

Clarity is at the heart of effective communication. When messages are clear and concise, they are more likely to be understood and acted upon. Leaders must strive to communicate their vision, goals, and expectations in a manner that leaves no room for ambiguity.

Simplify Your Message

Avoid jargon and complex language. Use simple, straightforward words that everyone can understand. The goal is to convey your message as clearly as possible.

Be Specific

Provide concrete details and examples to support your message. This helps eliminate confusion and ensures that everyone is on the same page.

Organize Your Thoughts

Structure your communication logically. Start with the main point, followed by supporting information, and conclude with a clear call to action or summary.

Seek Feedback

Encourage questions and feedback to ensure that your message has been understood. This also provides an opportunity to clarify any points that may have been misunderstood.

Example: When Steve Jobs introduced the first iPhone, he used simple, clear language to describe its revolutionary features. This clarity helped the audience understand the significance of the product and its potential impact on the market.

C. Active Listening

Active listening is a critical component of effective communication. It involves fully concentrating on the speaker, understanding the message, and responding thoughtfully. Active listening fosters trust, builds rapport, and ensures that communication is a two-way street.

Pay Attention

Give the speaker your full attention. Avoid distractions and maintain eye contact to show that you are engaged.

Show That You're Listening

Use verbal and non-verbal cues, such as nodding and smiling, to demonstrate that you are paying attention. Reflective listening, such as paraphrasing what the speaker has said, can also show understanding.

Provide Feedback

Summarize or paraphrase the speaker's message to ensure understanding. Ask questions for clarification and provide thoughtful responses.

Defer Judgment

Avoid interrupting or jumping to conclusions. Allow the speaker to finish his or her thoughts before responding.

Case Study

Richard Branson, the founder of Virgin Group, is known for his exceptional listening skills. He often emphasizes the importance of listening to employees, customers, and partners to understand their needs and concerns, which has been a key factor in Virgin's success.

D. Non-Verbal Communication

Non-verbal communication, including body language, facial expressions, and tone of voice, plays a significant role in how messages are perceived. Leaders must be aware of their non-verbal cues to ensure they are conveying the intended message.

Body Language

Maintain an open posture, use hand gestures to emphasize points, and avoid crossing your arms, which can be perceived as defensive.

Facial Expressions

Ensure your facial expressions match your words. Smiling can convey friendliness and approachability while frowning can indicate displeasure or confusion.

Tone of Voice

Your tone of voice can convey a range of emotions, from enthusiasm to frustration. Be mindful of your tone and adjust it to match the context of your message.

Eye Contact

Maintain appropriate eye contact to show interest and confidence. However, be mindful of cultural differences, as eye contact norms can vary.

Example: Oprah Winfrey's success as a communicator is partly due to her mastery of non-verbal communication. Her warm smile, open body language, and empathetic tone have made her a beloved figure and a powerful communicator.

E. Clear and Concise Messaging

Clear and concise messaging is essential for effective communication, especially in a fast-paced business environment. Leaders must be able to convey their messages quickly and clearly without losing the core essence.

Brevity is Key

Aim to be as brief as possible without sacrificing the completeness of your message. Avoid unnecessary details and focus on the main points.

Use Bullet Points

When communicating complex information, bullet points can help break down the content into manageable chunks, making it easier for the audience to grasp.

Avoid Overloading Information

Too much information at once can overwhelm your audience. Prioritize the most important points and deliver them in a structured manner.

Review and Edit

Always review and edit your messages for clarity and brevity. Eliminate redundant words and ensure that your message is easy to understand.

Example: Twitter's 280-character limit forces users to be concise. This constraint has taught many to convey their thoughts in a clear and succinct manner, making it an excellent practice for business communication.

F. Feedback and Constructive Criticism

Providing feedback and constructive criticism is a vital part of effective leadership. It helps team members grow, improves performance, and fosters a culture of continuous improvement.

Timely Feedback

Provide feedback as soon as possible after the observed behaviour or performance. Timely feedback is more impactful and relevant.

Be Specific and Objective

Focus on specific behaviours or outcomes rather than generalizations. Use concrete examples to illustrate your points.

Balanced Approach

Balance positive feedback with areas for improvement. Acknowledging strengths before discussing weaknesses can make the recipient more receptive.

Focus on Improvement

Frame criticism as an opportunity for growth. Offer actionable suggestions and support to help the individual improve.

Active Listening

Encourage a dialogue and listen to the recipient's perspective. This fosters a collaborative approach to development.

Example: Netflix's culture of feedback emphasizes radical candor, where employees are encouraged to give and receive honest feedback. This has created a high-performance culture that values continuous improvement.

G. The Role of Technology

In today's digital age, technology plays a crucial role in communication. Leaders must leverage technology effectively to enhance communication while being mindful of its potential pitfalls.

Email and Messaging

Use email and messaging platforms for clear and concise written communication. Be mindful of tone and ensure messages are well-structured.

Video Conferencing

Utilize video conferencing tools for face-to-face communication with remote teams. Ensure a professional setting, good lighting, and clear audio to enhance the experience.

Collaboration Tools

Leverage project management and collaboration tools to streamline communication and keep everyone on the same page. These tools can help track progress, share updates, and facilitate teamwork.

Social Media

Use social media platforms to communicate with a broader audience, share updates, and engage with stakeholders. Be mindful of maintaining a professional and consistent tone.

Example: Slack, a popular collaboration tool, has transformed the way teams communicate. Its real-time messaging, file sharing, and integration capabilities have made it easier for teams to collaborate effectively, regardless of location.

H. The Importance of Grammar and Syntax in Communication

Grammar and syntax form the foundation of clear and effective communication. Proper grammar ensures that sentences are structured correctly, facilitating the accurate transmission of ideas. It helps avoid misunderstandings that can arise from ambiguous or incorrect sentence construction. For instance, the placement of a comma can drastically change the meaning of a sentence, as in the classic example, "Let's eat, grandma" versus "Let's eat grandma." Such nuances highlight the critical role grammar plays in maintaining clarity and precision in both written and spoken communication.

Syntax, the arrangement of words and phrases to create well-formed sentences, further enhances the readability and coherence of communication. It allows the speaker or writer to convey his or her message in a logical and organized manner, making it easier for the audience to follow and understand the intended meaning. A well-structured sentence not only improves comprehension but also reflects the speaker's or writer's professionalism and attention to detail. In professional and academic settings, adherence to proper grammar and syntax is essential, as it demonstrates credibility and respect for the audience. In summary, mastering grammar and syntax is crucial for effective communication, enabling individuals to express their ideas clearly, accurately, and persuasively.

I. Conclusion

Effective communication is a cornerstone of successful leadership. By mastering the principles of clarity, active listening, non-verbal communication, clear and concise messaging, feedback and constructive criticism, and leveraging technology, leaders can foster a culture of openness, collaboration, and mutual respect. These skills not only enhance team performance but also build trust and strengthen relationships within the organization.

As you continue to develop your communication skills, remember that effective communication is an ongoing process. Continuously seek feedback, adapt your approach, and strive to improve. By doing so, you will become a more effective and influential leader, capable of guiding your team to excellence.

In the next chapter, we will explore the importance of decision-making and problem-solving in leadership, and how to develop these critical skills to navigate the challenges and opportunities that arise in the business world.

CHAPTER 6

MOTIVATION AND EMPOWERMENT

"Consult not your fears but your hopes and your dreams. Think not about your frustrations, but about your unfulfilled potential. Concern yourself not with what you tried and failed in, but with what it is still possible for you to do." – Pope John XXIII

"People work for money but go the extra mile for recognition, praise and rewards." --Dale Carnegie

A. Introduction

Motivation and empowerment are essential components of effective leadership. A motivated and empowered team is more engaged, productive, and committed to achieving organizational goals. As a leader, understanding how to inspire, delegate, recognize, and reward your team can significantly impact their performance and job satisfaction. This chapter delves into the strategies and principles that leaders can employ to foster a motivated and empowered workforce.

B. Inspiring Your Team

Inspiration is the driving force that propels individuals to go above and beyond in their roles. To inspire your team, you must create an environment that fosters enthusiasm, creativity, and a sense of purpose.

Lead by Example

Demonstrate the behaviours and attitudes you expect from your team. Show dedication, integrity, and a strong work ethic to inspire similar traits in others.

Communicate a Clear Vision

Articulate a compelling vision that aligns with the team's values and goals. Help team members understand how their work contributes to the larger picture, providing them with a sense of purpose and direction.

Encourage Innovation

Foster a culture where new ideas are welcomed and valued. Encourage team members to think creatively and take calculated risks, knowing that their contributions are appreciated.

Provide Support and Resources

Ensure that your team has the tools, resources, and support it needs to succeed. Removing obstacles and providing guidance can significantly boost team members' confidence and motivation.

Example: Elon Musk's vision for SpaceX to make space travel more affordable and eventually enable human life on Mars has inspired his team to push the boundaries of technology and innovation.

C. Delegation and Trust

Effective delegation and trust are crucial for empowering your team. By entrusting team members with responsibilities, you not only free up your own time but also build their confidence and skills.

Assign Meaningful Tasks

Delegate tasks that are challenging and meaningful, allowing team members to grow and develop their skills. Ensure that the tasks align with their strengths and career goals.

Provide Autonomy

Give your team the autonomy to make decisions and take ownership of their work. Trusting them to handle tasks independently fosters a sense of responsibility and accountability.

Offer Guidance, Not Micromanagement

Provide clear instructions and expectations, but avoid micromanaging. Be available for support and guidance, but allow your team the space to find its own solutions.

Build Trust

Trust is a two-way street. Show trust in your team's abilities and integrity, and work to earn its trust through transparency, consistency, and reliability.

Case Study

Google's "20% time" policy, which allows employees to spend 20% of their time on projects of their own choosing, has led to the development of innovative products like Gmail and Google News. This policy demonstrates trust and encourages creativity and ownership.

D. Empowerment through Training and Development

Continuous learning and development are essential for empowering employees. By investing in their growth, leaders can help their team members reach their full potential and stay motivated.

Identify Training Needs

Regularly assess the skills and knowledge gaps within your team. Offer training programs that address these gaps and enhance their abilities.

Provide Access to Resources

Ensure your team has access to the necessary resources, such as books, online courses, workshops, and seminars, to support their learning.

Encourage Self-Directed Learning

Motivate team members to take charge of their own development. Encourage them to seek out learning opportunities and set personal growth goals.

Mentorship and Coaching

Pair team members with mentors or coaches who can provide guidance, share experiences, and offer support in their professional development.

Example: IBM's extensive training programs, such as their Think Academy, offer employees opportunities to learn new skills and advance their careers. This commitment to employee development has helped IBM maintain a skilled and motivated workforce.

E. Recognition and Rewards

Recognition and rewards are powerful motivators that can significantly enhance team morale and performance. Acknowledging and rewarding team members for their hard work and achievements fosters a positive work environment.

Timely and Specific Recognition

Recognize and appreciate efforts and accomplishments as soon as they occur. Be specific about what the individual did well and how it contributed to the team's success.

Personalized Rewards

Tailor rewards to the preferences and interests of your team members. Personalized rewards demonstrate that you value and understand their individual contributions and needs.

Celebrate Milestones and Achievements

Celebrate both small and large milestones. Regular celebrations of achievements help maintain a positive atmosphere and keep motivation levels high.

Provide Growth Opportunities

Offer opportunities for professional development and career advancement as rewards. This not only recognizes their current contributions but also invests in their future potential.

Example: At Zappos, the online shoe retailer, employee recognition is a core part of the company culture. They have a dedicated peer-to-peer recognition program called "Zollars" where employees can recognize each other's contributions, which can be redeemed for rewards.

F. Building a Collaborative Environment

Collaboration is key to a motivated and empowered team. By fostering a collaborative environment, leaders can harness the collective strengths and talents of their team members.

Encourage Teamwork

Promote a culture of teamwork and collaboration. Encourage team members to work together on projects, share ideas, and support each other.

Facilitate Open Communication

Create an open communication environment where team members feel comfortable sharing their thoughts and feedback. Regular team meetings and open-door policies can help achieve this.

Leverage Diverse Perspectives

Value and leverage the diverse perspectives within your team. Encourage team members to share their unique insights and experiences, which can lead to innovative solutions.

Recognize Collaborative Efforts

Acknowledge and reward collaborative efforts and team achievements. This reinforces the importance of working together and fosters a sense of community.

Case Study

Pixar's open office layout and regular brainstorming sessions encourage collaboration and the exchange of ideas among employees. This collaborative culture has been a driving force behind Pixar's creative success and innovation in the animation industry.

G. Conclusion

Motivation and empowerment are fundamental to effective leadership and the overall success of any organization. By inspiring your team, delegating with trust, investing in their development, recognizing their efforts, and fostering a collaborative environment, you create an atmosphere where individuals feel valued, motivated, and empowered to perform at their best. These practices not only enhance productivity and job satisfaction but also foster loyalty and a positive organizational culture.

As you continue to develop your leadership skills, remember that motivation and empowerment are ongoing processes. Continuously seek ways to inspire, support, and recognize your team, and you will build a high-performing, engaged, and loyal workforce capable of achieving excellence.

In the next chapter, we will explore the critical aspects of Change Management including strategies for leading change, and maintaining morale during transitions.

PART III

LEADING THROUGH CHALLENGES

CHAPTER 7

CHANGE MANAGEMENT

"Everyone agrees that change management is important. Making it happen effectively, however, needs to be a core competence of managers and not something that they can pass off to others." – Ron Ashkenas

A. Introduction

Change is an inevitable part of any organization's lifecycle. Whether it's a shift in market dynamics, technological advancements, or internal restructuring, the ability to manage change effectively is crucial for sustaining success. Change management involves the process, tools, and techniques used to manage the people side of change to achieve the required business outcomes. This chapter explores the fundamental strategies for leading change, overcoming resistance, and maintaining morale during transitions.

B. Strategies for Leading Change

Leading change requires a strategic approach that involves careful planning, clear communication, and strong leadership. Here are some key strategies to effectively lead change:

Establish a Clear Vision and Goals

Clearly define the vision and objectives of the change. Ensure that all team members understand the purpose and benefits of the change, and how it aligns with the organization's overall mission and goals.

Create a Detailed Plan

Develop a comprehensive change management plan that outlines the steps, timelines, resources, and responsibilities involved. This plan should include contingency measures to address potential challenges and setbacks.

Communicate Transparently

Maintain open and honest communication throughout the change process. Provide regular updates, address concerns, and encourage feedback from team members. Transparent communication helps build trust and reduces uncertainty.

Engage and Involve Employees

Involve employees in the change process by seeking their input and participation. This not only enhances buy-in and commitment but also leverages their insights and expertise.

Provide Training and Support

Offer training and support to help employees adapt to new systems, processes, or roles. Equip them with the necessary skills and knowledge to navigate the change successfully.

Case Study

When Microsoft transitioned to a cloud-first strategy under CEO Satya Nadella, the company established a clear vision and goals, communicated transparently with employees, provided extensive training, and actively engaged its workforce in the transformation process. This strategic approach led to a successful transition and revitalized the company's growth.

C. Overcoming Resistance

Resistance to change is a natural human response. Understanding and addressing this resistance is crucial for the success of any change initiative. Here are some strategies to overcome resistance:

Understand the Root Causes

Identify the underlying reasons for resistance. These could include fear of the unknown, loss of control, perceived threats to job security, or lack of trust in leadership. Addressing these root causes can help mitigate resistance.

Build Trust and Credibility

Trust in leadership plays a significant role in overcoming resistance. Demonstrate competence, reliability, and integrity to build trust and credibility with your team.

Involve Key Influencers

Identify and involve key influencers within the organization who can champion the change and positively influence their peers. Their support can help sway opinion and reduce resistance.

Address Concerns and Provide Reassurance

Listen to employees' concerns and provide reassurance. Clarify misconceptions, highlight the benefits of the change, and offer support to alleviate fears.

Implement Change Gradually

Whenever possible, implement change gradually rather than abruptly. A phased approach allows employees to adjust incrementally and reduces the shock and resistance associated with sudden changes.

Example: When Procter & Gamble (P&G) faced resistance during a major organizational restructuring, they involved key influencers from various departments, communicated transparently about the reasons for the change, and provided continuous support and reassurance. This approach helped reduce resistance and facilitated a smoother transition.

D. Maintaining Morale During Transitions

Maintaining employee morale during periods of change is essential to ensure productivity and engagement. Here are some strategies to keep morale high during transitions:

Recognize and Acknowledge Efforts

Recognize and appreciate the efforts and contributions of employees throughout the change process. Acknowledgement and appreciation go a long way in boosting morale.

Maintain Open Communication

Keep communication channels open and provide regular updates on the progress of the change. Address any rumors or misinformation promptly to prevent anxiety and confusion.

Promote a Positive Work Environment

Foster a supportive and positive work environment. Encourage team collaboration, provide opportunities for social interaction, and ensure that employees have access to necessary resources and support.

Offer Professional Development Opportunities:

Provide opportunities for employees to learn new skills and advance their careers. Professional development initiatives demonstrate investment in employees' growth and can enhance their morale.

Encourage Work-Life Balance

Support employees in maintaining a healthy work-life balance during transitions. Flexible work arrangements and wellness programs can help reduce stress and improve overall well-being.

Case Study

During its transition to agile methodologies, Spotify maintained employee morale by promoting a positive work environment, recognizing efforts, and offering continuous learning opportunities. These efforts helped keep employees engaged and motivated throughout the change process.

E. Conclusion

Change management is a critical leadership skill that involves guiding an organization through transitions while minimizing disruption and maintaining productivity. By implementing effective strategies for leading change, overcoming resistance, and maintaining morale, leaders can ensure a smoother and more successful transformation. Remember that change is an ongoing process, and continuous communication, support, and adaptation are key to sustaining positive outcomes.

As you continue your leadership journey, embrace change as an opportunity for growth and innovation. By mastering the art of change management, you can lead your team with confidence, resilience, and a shared vision for the future. In the next chapter, we will explore the importance of conflict resolution as a key element in effective leadership.

CHAPTER 8

CONFLICT RESOLUTION

"When you have a conflict, that means that there are truths that have to be addressed on each side of the conflict. And when you have a conflict, then it's an educational process to try to resolve the conflict. And to resolve that, you have to get people on both sides of the conflict involved so that they can dialogue." – Dolores Huerta

A. Introduction

Conflict is an inevitable aspect of any organization. Differences in opinions, goals, and perspectives can lead to disagreements and tensions among team members. However, when managed effectively, conflict can lead to growth, innovation, and stronger relationships. This chapter explores the nature of conflict in the workplace, strategies for identifying sources of conflict, mediation techniques, and ways to turn conflict into an opportunity for positive change.

B. Identifying Sources of Conflict

Understanding the root causes of conflict is the first step in resolving it. Conflicts can arise from a variety of sources, including:

Communication Breakdown

Misunderstandings, lack of communication, or misinterpretation of information can lead to conflicts. Clear and effective communication is crucial to prevent such issues.

Diverging Goals and Priorities

When team members have different objectives or priorities, conflicts can arise. Ensuring alignment and clarity of goals can help mitigate this.

Personality Clashes

Differences in personality, work style, and values can lead to conflicts. Recognizing and respecting individual differences is essential for a harmonious workplace.

Resource Scarcity

Competition for limited resources such as budget, time, or personnel can cause conflicts. Transparent and fair allocation of resources can help reduce tensions.

Role Ambiguity

Unclear roles and responsibilities can lead to confusion and conflict. Clearly defining and communicating roles can prevent misunderstandings.

Perceived Inequity

Feelings of unfair treatment or favouritism can lead to resentment and conflict. Ensuring fairness and equity in the workplace is vital.

Example: In a software development team, a conflict arose owing to unclear roles and responsibilities, leading to duplicated efforts and missed deadlines. By clearly defining roles and improving communication, the team was able to resolve the conflict and improve its collaboration.

C. Mediation Techniques

Effective mediation techniques can help resolve conflicts constructively. Here are some key techniques for mediating conflicts:

Active Listening

Encourage all parties to express their viewpoints and listen actively. Acknowledge their feelings and concerns without interrupting or judging.

Empathy and Understanding

Show empathy and strive to understand the perspectives of all parties involved. Validating their feelings can help build trust and openness.

Neutral Facilitation

As a mediator, remain neutral and impartial. Facilitate the discussion without taking sides, and ensure that everyone has an equal opportunity to speak.

Define the Problem

Clearly define the problem and the underlying issues. Ensure that all parties agree on what the conflict is about before moving forward.

Explore Solutions

Encourage brainstorming and explore potential solutions together. Focus on finding mutually acceptable solutions rather than assigning blame.

Agree on Action Steps

Once a solution is identified, agree on specific action steps and responsibilities. Ensure that all parties are committed to the resolution plan.

Follow-Up

Monitor the progress of the resolution and follow up with the parties involved. Address any lingering issues or concerns promptly.

Case Study

In a marketing team, a conflict arose between two members over the allocation of project responsibilities. The team leader facilitated a mediation session, actively listened to both parties and helped them understand each other's perspectives. By defining the problem and exploring solutions together, they reached an agreement and improved their working relationship.

D. Turning Conflict into Opportunity

Conflict can be an opportunity for growth and improvement if approached with the right mindset. Here's how to turn conflict into a positive force:

Encourage Open Dialogue

Foster a culture of open dialogue where team members feel comfortable expressing their opinions and concerns. Open communication can prevent conflicts from escalating and promote mutual understanding.

Learn from Conflict

Analyze conflicts to understand their root causes and identify areas for improvement. Use conflicts as learning opportunities to enhance processes, communication, and team dynamics.

Strengthen Relationships

Resolving conflicts constructively can strengthen relationships and build trust among team members. It demonstrates that differences can be addressed respectfully and collaboratively.

Drive Innovation

Conflicts often arise from differing viewpoints and ideas. Embrace these differences as opportunities for innovation and creative problem-solving.

Enhance Problem-Solving Skills

Managing conflicts effectively can improve your problem-solving skills and those of your team. It fosters resilience and adaptability in the face of challenges.

Promote Personal Growth

Encourage team members to reflect on their role in conflicts and identify areas for personal growth. Self-awareness and a willingness to improve can lead to more effective teamwork.

Example: In a product development team, a conflict over design choices led to an open discussion where all team members could voice their opinions. This dialogue resulted in a more innovative and customer-centric design, turning the initial conflict into a driver for better outcomes.

E. Conclusion

Conflict resolution is a vital leadership skill that requires empathy, active listening, and a commitment to finding constructive solutions. By identifying the sources of conflict, employing effective mediation techniques, and viewing conflict as an opportunity for growth, leaders can foster a positive and collaborative work environment.

Remember that conflict, when managed well, can lead to stronger relationships, innovative ideas, and continuous improvement. Embrace conflicts as opportunities to enhance communication, build trust, and drive your team towards greater success.

As you continue your leadership journey, prioritize conflict resolution as a key aspect of your leadership toolkit. In the next chapter, we will explore the importance of crisis management and how it can benefit your team and the organization.

CHAPTER 9

CRISIS MANAGEMENT

"I really do think that any deep crisis is an opportunity to make your life extraordinary in some way." --Martha Beck

A. Introduction

In the dynamic world of business, crises are inevitable. Whether it's a financial downturn, a natural disaster, a public relations nightmare, or a sudden operational failure, crises test the resilience and preparedness of organizations. Effective crisis management is crucial for mitigating damage, maintaining trust, and steering the organization back to stability. This chapter explores the essentials of crisis management, strategies for handling crises, and the leadership skills necessary to navigate turbulent times.

B. Understanding Crises

Before diving into crisis management strategies, it's important to understand the nature of crises and their potential impact on organizations. Crises can be categorized into several types:

Natural Crises

These are events such as earthquakes, floods, hurricanes, or pandemics that disrupt normal business operations.

Technological Crises:

Failures in technology, such as data breaches, software malfunctions, or infrastructure breakdowns are referred to as technological crises.

Financial Crises

Economic downturns, bankruptcy, or sudden financial losses that threaten the stability of the organization are known as financial crises.

Human Crises

Human crises refer to issues related to personnel, such as workplace violence, strikes, or key personnel departures.

Reputational Crises

These refer to events that damage the public perception of the organization, such as scandals, negative media coverage, or customer backlash.

C. Crisis Preparedness

Preparation is the cornerstone of effective crisis management. Being proactive can significantly reduce the impact of a crisis. Key steps for crisis preparedness include:

Risk Assessment

Identify potential risks and vulnerabilities within the organization. Conduct regular assessments to stay updated on emerging threats.

Crisis Plan Development

Develop a comprehensive crisis management plan that outlines procedures, roles, and responsibilities during a crisis. Ensure that the plan is flexible to adapt to various scenarios.

Communication Plan

Establish a clear communication strategy for internal and external stakeholders. Designate spokespersons and develop templates for timely and accurate communication.

Training and Drills

Conduct regular training sessions and crisis simulations for employees to ensure they understand their roles and can respond effectively under pressure.

Resource Allocation

Ensure that the necessary resources, such as emergency funds, technology, and personnel, are readily available to handle crises.

D. Immediate Response Strategies

When a crisis strikes, immediate and decisive action is required. Effective response strategies include:

Activate the Crisis Management Team

Mobilize a pre-designated crisis management team responsible for executing the crisis plan. Ensure that team members understand their roles and responsibilities.

Assess the Situation

Quickly gather accurate information to understand the scope and impact of the crisis. Make data-driven decisions based on reliable sources.

Communicate Transparently

Maintain open and honest communication with stakeholders. Provide regular updates, acknowledge the situation, and outline the steps being taken to address the crisis.

Prioritize Safety

Ensure the safety and well-being of employees, customers, and other stakeholders. Implement necessary measures to protect people and assets.

Manage Public Relations

Address media inquiries and public concerns promptly. Control the narrative by providing accurate information and demonstrating accountability.

E. Long-Term Recovery

After the immediate response, the focus shifts to recovery and rebuilding. Key elements of long-term recovery include:

Business Continuity Planning

Develop and implement plans to resume normal operations as quickly as possible. Identify critical functions and prioritize their restoration.

Financial Management

Assess the financial impact of the crisis and develop strategies for recovery. Explore options such as loans, grants, or insurance claims to stabilize the organization.

Reputation Management

You never know the importance of reputation until you lose it. Work to rebuild trust and credibility with stakeholders. Address any lingering concerns, demonstrate transparency, and highlight positive actions taken during the crisis.

Employee Support

Provide support to employees who may have been affected by the crisis. Offer counseling, resources, and opportunities for involvement in the recovery process.

Learning and Improvement

Conduct a thorough review of the crisis response to identify strengths and areas for improvement. Update crisis management plans based on lessons learned.

F. Leadership in Crisis

Effective leadership is critical during a crisis. Leaders must demonstrate the following qualities:

Calm and Composure

Maintain a calm demeanor to reassure stakeholders and make rational decisions.

Decisiveness

Make timely and informed decisions, even in the face of uncertainty. Clearly communicate decisions and their rationale.

Empathy

Show empathy and understanding towards those affected by the crisis. Address their concerns and provide support.

Transparency

Be transparent in communication and actions. Build trust by being honest and accountable.

Resilience

Exhibit resilience and determination to overcome challenges and guide the organization towards recovery.

G. Turning Crisis into Opportunity

Crises, while challenging, can also present opportunities for growth and improvement:

Innovation

Crises often necessitate creative solutions. Encourage innovation and flexibility to adapt to new circumstances.

Strengthened Relationships

Effective crisis management can strengthen relationships with stakeholders by demonstrating reliability and trustworthiness.

Enhanced Resilience

Learn from the crisis to build greater resilience. Implement improvements to prevent future crises and enhance preparedness.

Positive Change

Use the crisis as a catalyst for positive organizational change. Address underlying issues and drive improvements in processes and culture.

Case Study

When a major cyberattack hit GlobalLogistics, a leading international shipping company, the entire organization was thrown into chaos. Systems were down, shipments were delayed, and customer trust was at risk. John Davis, the Chief Operating Officer, immediately took charge of the crisis. Recognizing the urgency, John quickly assembled a cross-functional crisis management team that included IT, communications, legal, and operations leaders. He ensured clear, transparent communication with employees, customers, and stakeholders, acknowledging the issue and outlining the steps being taken to resolve it.

John's calm demeanour and decisive actions reassured the team, allowing members to focus on solutions rather than panic. He prioritized restoring critical systems while simultaneously coordinating with cybersecurity experts to secure the network and prevent further breaches. John also led the effort to communicate with customers, offering compensation for delays and maintaining their trust through honesty and accountability.

Thanks to John's leadership, GlobalLogistics not only recovered from the crisis but emerged stronger, with improved cybersecurity measures and enhanced crisis response protocols. His ability to manage the situation with clarity, speed, and empathy exemplified effective crisis management, turning a potential disaster into an opportunity for growth and resilience.

H. Conclusion

Crisis management is an essential component of effective leadership. By understanding the nature of crises, preparing proactively, responding decisively, and leading with empathy and transparency, leaders can navigate their organizations through turbulent times. Remember, every crisis, while challenging, also presents an opportunity for growth, innovation, and strengthening the fabric of the organization.

As you continue your leadership journey, embrace the principles of crisis management to ensure that you are well-equipped to handle whatever challenges come your way. In the next chapter, we will explore the importance of having a clear vision and aligning the team with that vision, and how it can drive long-term success for your team and organization.

PART IV

STRATEGIC LEADERSHIP

CHAPTER 10

VISIONARY LEADERSHIP

*The visionary starts with a clean sheet of paper, and re-imagines the world. -
-Malcolm Gladwell*

A. Introduction

Visionary leadership is a critical element in guiding an organization toward long-term success and innovation. Visionary leaders possess the ability to see beyond the immediate horizon, imagining a future that others might not yet perceive. They inspire their teams to work towards this future with enthusiasm and dedication. This chapter explores the key aspects of visionary leadership, including setting a clear vision, aligning your team with that vision, the importance of long-term planning, fostering innovation, and maintaining flexibility.

B. Setting a Clear Vision

A clear and compelling vision is the cornerstone of visionary leadership. It provides a sense of direction and purpose, serving as a guiding star for the organization. To set a clear vision, leaders must:

Understand the Landscape

Analyze industry trends, competitive dynamics, and internal capabilities to identify opportunities and challenges.

Articulate the Vision

Clearly define the long-term goals and aspirations of the organization. Ensure the vision is specific, achievable, and inspiring.

Communicate Effectively

Share the vision with the organization through various channels. Use storytelling to make the vision relatable and compelling.

Be Authentic

Ensure the vision aligns with the leader's values and the core values of the organization. Authenticity builds trust and commitment.

C. Aligning Your Team with the Vision

Once the vision is set, it is crucial to align the team with this vision. This alignment ensures that everyone in the organization is working towards the same goals. Key steps include:

Engage and Involve

Involve team members in the vision-setting process. Solicit their input and feedback to foster a sense of ownership and commitment.

Set Clear Objectives

Break down the vision into specific, measurable, achievable, relevant, and time-bound (SMART) objectives for different teams and individuals.

Communicate Continuously

Regularly communicate progress towards the vision. Use meetings, newsletters, and other communication tools to keep the vision top-of-mind.

Empower and Support

Provide the necessary resources, training, and support to help team members contribute effectively to the vision. Empower them to take initiative and innovate.

D. Long-Term Planning

Visionary leadership requires a focus on long-term planning. This involves anticipating future trends, preparing for potential challenges, and ensuring the organization is equipped to achieve its vision. Effective long-term planning includes:

Strategic Planning

Develop a strategic plan that outlines the steps needed to achieve the vision. Include short-term, medium-term, and long-term goals, and regularly review and adjust the plan as necessary.

Resource Allocation

Allocate resources, including finances, personnel, and technology, to support the strategic plan. Ensure that resources are used efficiently and effectively.

Risk Management

Identify potential risks and develop contingency plans. Prepare the organization to respond swiftly to unforeseen challenges.

Innovation and Adaptation

Foster a culture of innovation and continuous improvement. Encourage the team to experiment, learn, and adapt to changing circumstances.

E. Fostering Innovation

Innovation is a key component of visionary leadership. Visionary leaders encourage creativity and experimentation within their teams. To foster innovation:

Create a Safe Environment

Build a culture where employees feel safe to share new ideas and take risks without fear of failure.

Encourage Collaboration

Promote cross-functional collaboration to bring diverse perspectives and expertise to the table.

Invest in Learning and Development

Provide ongoing training and development opportunities to keep the team's skills and knowledge up-to-date.

Reward Innovation

Recognize and reward innovative ideas and successful implementations to motivate continued creativity.

F. Maintaining Flexibility

A visionary leader must also be flexible and adaptable. The ability to pivot and adjust the vision and strategy in response to changing circumstances is crucial. To maintain flexibility:

Monitor Progress

Regularly review and assess progress towards the vision. Be open to feedback and willing to make adjustments as needed.

Stay Informed

Keep abreast of industry trends, technological advancements, and external factors that could impact the vision and strategy.

Encourage Agility

Foster an agile mindset within the team, where change is embraced, and new opportunities are quickly seized.

Be Resilient

Develop resilience in yourself and your team to withstand setbacks and bounce back stronger.

Case Study

Emily Chen, the visionary founder and CEO of GreenFuture Energy, transformed the renewable energy industry through her foresight and innovative thinking. Years before the global shift toward sustainable energy became mainstream, Emily recognized the urgent need to address climate change and saw the potential for solar and wind energy to power the future. She founded GreenFuture Energy with a bold vision: to make renewable energy affordable and accessible to everyone, including underserved communities.

Emily's leadership was marked by her ability to anticipate industry trends and technological advancements. She invested heavily in research and development, pushing her team to explore new technologies like advanced solar panels and energy storage systems. Her commitment to innovation and sustainability attracted top talent and investors who shared her vision.

Under Emily's leadership, GreenFuture Energy not only pioneered several groundbreaking technologies but also expanded rapidly into global markets. She forged partnerships with governments and NGOs, ensuring that her vision of a sustainable future was realized on a large scale. Emily's ability to see beyond current market demands and inspire others to share her vision made her a true visionary leader, driving both her company and the renewable energy industry toward a brighter, greener future.

G. Conclusion

Visionary leadership is about seeing beyond the present and guiding the organization toward a brighter future. By setting a clear vision, aligning the team, focusing on long-term planning, fostering innovation, and maintaining flexibility, visionary leaders can inspire and motivate their teams to achieve extraordinary results. The ability to envision and pursue a bold future is what sets great leaders apart, enabling them to drive their organizations to new heights of success and innovation.

As you continue your leadership journey, embrace the principles of visionary leadership to ensure that you are well-equipped to handle whatever challenges come your way. In the next chapter, we will explore the importance of fostering a culture of continuous improvement and how it can drive long-term success for your team and organization.

CHAPTER 11

INNOVATION AND CREATIVITY

"You can't use up creativity. The more you use, the more you have."
--Maya Angelou

"Creativity is thinking up new things. Innovation is doing new things."
--Theodore Levitt

A. Introduction

In today's rapidly changing business environment, innovation and creativity are essential for organizations to stay competitive and relevant. Innovation is about bringing new ideas to life, while creativity is the ability to think beyond conventional boundaries. Together, they drive progress, fuel growth, and enable companies to solve complex problems. This chapter explores the significance of innovation and creativity, provides practical strategies to foster them within your organization, and presents case studies of companies that have successfully harnessed these qualities.

B. The Importance of Innovation and Creativity

Innovation and creativity are the lifeblood of any successful organization. They lead to the development of new products, services, and processes that can differentiate a company from its competitors. Here are some key reasons why innovation and creativity are vital:

Driving Growth

Innovative ideas can lead to new revenue streams and market opportunities.

Enhancing Competitiveness

Creativity helps organizations stay ahead of the curve by continuously improving and adapting.

Solving Problems

Innovative solutions can address complex challenges and inefficiencies.

Employee Engagement

A culture of creativity fosters employee satisfaction and motivation, as team members feel their ideas are valued.

C. Fostering a Culture of Innovation and Creativity

Creating an environment where innovation and creativity can thrive requires deliberate effort and strategic initiatives. Here are some strategies to foster such a culture:

Encourage Risk-Taking

Create a safe environment where employees feel comfortable taking risks and experimenting with new ideas without fear of failure.

Promote Collaboration

Facilitate cross-functional collaboration to leverage diverse perspectives and expertise.

Provide Resources

Allocate time, budget, and tools for employees to explore and develop innovative ideas.

Recognize and Reward

Acknowledge and reward innovative efforts to motivate continuous creativity.

Leadership Support

Ensure that leadership actively supports and champions innovation initiatives.

D. Strategies for Implementing Innovation

To effectively implement innovation, organizations need a structured approach. Key strategies include:

Idea Generation

Encourage brainstorming sessions, idea challenges, and hackathons to generate a pool of innovative ideas.

Idea Evaluation

Establish criteria to assess the feasibility, impact, and alignment of ideas with organizational goals.

Prototyping and Testing

Develop prototypes and conduct pilot tests to refine ideas before full-scale implementation.

Scaling Innovation

Once validated, scale successful innovations across the organization.

Continuous Improvement

Continuously monitor and refine innovations to ensure they deliver sustained value.

Case Studies

Google's 20% Time Policy

Google is renowned for its culture of innovation, and one of the key drivers of this culture is its "20% Time" policy. This policy allows employees to spend 20% of their work time on projects that interest them, even if these projects are not part of their regular job responsibilities. This approach has led to the development of some of Google's most successful products, including Gmail and Google News.

Key Takeaways:

» **Empower Employees**: Allowing employees to explore their passions can lead to groundbreaking innovations.
» **Foster Autonomy**: Providing autonomy and trust can enhance creativity and job satisfaction.

3M's Innovation Culture

3M, a global conglomerate known for its innovative products, has a long-standing commitment to fostering a culture of creativity. The company encourages its employees to spend 15% of their time on experimental projects. This freedom has led to the invention of numerous successful products, such as the Post-it Note.

Key Takeaways:

» **Encourage Experimentation**: Allocating time for experimentation can result in the development of unique and valuable products.

» **Support from Leadership**: Leadership commitment to innovation is crucial for sustaining a creative culture.

E. Conclusion

Innovation and creativity are indispensable for organizations striving for long-term success and adaptability in a dynamic business landscape. By fostering a culture that encourages risk-taking, collaboration, and continuous learning, leaders can unlock the full potential of their teams and drive transformative growth. The examples of Google and 3M illustrate that with the right environment and support, remarkable innovations can emerge. As you continue to lead and inspire your team, remember that nurturing creativity and innovation is an ongoing journey that requires commitment and strategic effort.

CHAPTER 12

DECISION-MAKING AND PROBLEM-SOLVING

"In any moment of decision, the best thing you can do is the right thing, the next best thing is the wrong thing, and the worst thing you can do is nothing." --Theodore Roosevelt

"The biggest problem in the world could have been solved when it was small." - Witter Bynner

A. Introduction

Effective decision-making and problem-solving are critical skills for leaders in any organization. These skills enable leaders to navigate complex challenges, make informed choices, and drive the organization toward its goals. This chapter explores the importance of data-driven decisions, analytical thinking, and collaborative problem-solving. We will also examine a real-world case study to illustrate these concepts in action.

B. Data-Driven Decisions

Data-driven decision-making involves using data and analytics to inform and guide decisions. This approach minimizes biases, enhances accuracy, and leads to more objective outcomes. Key aspects of data-driven decision-making include:

Data Collection

Gather relevant data from various sources, including internal records, market research, and customer feedback.

Data Analysis

Use statistical and analytical tools to interpret the data and extract meaningful insights.

Decision Support Systems

Implement systems and software that facilitate data analysis and decision-making processes.

Continuous Monitoring

Regularly track and analyze data to make informed adjustments and improvements.

C. Analytical Thinking

Analytical thinking is the ability to systematically analyze information, identify patterns, and draw logical conclusions. It is essential for solving complex problems and making sound decisions. Key components of analytical thinking include:

Critical Thinking

Evaluate information critically, questioning assumptions and considering multiple perspectives.

Problem Decomposition

Break down complex problems into smaller, more manageable parts to understand their underlying components.

Root Cause Analysis

Identify the root causes of problems to address them effectively rather than merely treating symptoms.

Scenario Planning

Develop and evaluate different scenarios to anticipate potential outcomes and make informed choices.

D. Collaborative Problem-Solving

Collaborative problem-solving involves engaging team members in the decision-making process to leverage their collective knowledge and expertise. This approach fosters creativity, enhances buy-in, and leads to more robust solutions. Key elements of collaborative problem-solving include:

Diverse Teams

Assemble teams with diverse skills, backgrounds, and perspectives to enrich the problem-solving process.

Open Communication

Encourage open and transparent communication to share ideas and insights freely.

Brainstorming Sessions

Conduct brainstorming sessions to generate a wide range of ideas and potential solutions.

Consensus Building

Facilitate discussions and negotiations to reach a consensus on the best course of action.

E. Solution

Effective decision-making and problem-solving involve a structured approach to identifying, analyzing, and implementing solutions. The process typically includes the following steps:

Define the Problem

Clearly articulate the problem, its scope, and its impact on the organization.

Gather Information

Collect relevant data and information to understand the problem's context and underlying causes.

Generate Alternatives

Brainstorm and evaluate multiple solutions, considering their feasibility and potential impact.

Select the Best Solution

Choose the most suitable solution based on data analysis, expert input, and stakeholder feedback.

Implement the Solution

Develop an action plan to implement the chosen solution, assigning responsibilities and timelines.

Evaluate Results

Monitor and assess the effectiveness of the solution, making adjustments as needed to achieve desired outcomes.

F. Case Study: IBM's Decision-Making Transformation

Background: IBM, a global technology company, faced declining revenues and market share in the early 2010s because of rapidly changing technology trends and increased competition.

Problem: The company needed to make strategic decisions to pivot its business model and regain market leadership.

Data-Driven Decisions: IBM invested heavily in data analytics and artificial intelligence (AI) to gather insights from vast amounts of data. This allowed the company to identify emerging trends and customer needs accurately.

Analytical Thinking: The company applied analytical thinking to evaluate its existing product portfolio and identify areas for innovation. Its leaders conducted root cause analysis to understand why certain products were underperforming and developed scenarios to forecast future market conditions.

Collaborative Problem-Solving: IBM fostered a culture of collaboration by involving cross-functional teams in the decision-making process. It held brainstorming sessions and workshops to generate innovative ideas and solutions.

Solution: Based on its data-driven insights and collaborative efforts, IBM decided to shift its focus to cloud computing, AI, and other emerging technologies. It launched new products and services, restructured its operations, and formed strategic partnerships to accelerate its transformation.

Outcome: IBM's decision-making and problem-solving efforts led to a successful business transformation. The company regained its competitive edge, improved its financial performance, and established itself as a leader in cloud computing and AI.

G. Conclusion

Effective decision-making and problem-solving are fundamental to successful leadership. By leveraging data-driven decisions, analytical thinking, and collaborative problem-solving, leaders can navigate complex challenges and drive their organizations toward sustained success. The case study of IBM illustrates the power of these approaches in transforming a business and achieving strategic objectives.

As you develop your leadership skills, remember that decision-making and problem-solving are continuous processes that require ongoing learning, adaptation, and collaboration. In the next chapter, we will explore the importance of leadership development, focusing on mentorship and coaching.

PART V

LEADERSHIP AND DEVELOPMENT

CHAPTER 13

MENTORSHIP AND COACHING

"Mentors build mentors. Leaders build leaders. When you look at it closely, it's really one and the same thing." - Tony Dungy

"Probably my best quality as a coach is that I ask a lot of challenging questions and let the person come up with the answer." – Phil Dixon

A. Introduction

Mentorship and coaching are integral components of effective leadership, serving as the conduits through which knowledge, experience, and wisdom are passed down to future generations. These practices go beyond simple instruction; they are about cultivating potential, nurturing growth, and guiding individuals toward achieving their fullest capabilities. In today's fast-paced and ever-changing business environment, leaders must not only be competent in their own roles but also adept at fostering the development of others. This chapter delves into the essentials of mentorship and coaching, exploring how these practices can be leveraged to build a robust leadership pipeline and create a culture of continuous improvement.

B. Developing Future Leaders

The long-term success of any organization hinges on its ability to develop future leaders. Mentorship and coaching are critical in this process, as they provide emerging leaders with the guidance and support they need to navigate the complexities of their roles. Effective mentors not only share their knowledge and experience but also model the behaviours and values that are essential for leadership. They challenge their mentees to think critically, encouraging them to step outside their comfort zones and take on new challenges. By doing so, mentors help to build the confidence and competence of future leaders, ensuring that they are well-prepared to assume greater responsibilities.

In addition to traditional one-on-one mentoring relationships, organizations should consider implementing group mentoring programs and peer coaching networks. These approaches allow for the sharing of diverse perspectives and can accelerate the development of leadership skills across a broader swath of the organization. By fostering a culture of mentorship, organizations can ensure that leadership development is not confined to the upper echelons but is embedded throughout the entire organization.

C. Coaching Techniques

Coaching is a more structured and goal-oriented form of development compared to mentorship. While mentorship is often long-term and focused on overall growth, coaching is typically short-term and centered around specific skills or objectives. Effective coaching requires a deep understanding of both the individual being coached and the specific outcomes desired. Here are some key coaching techniques that can be employed:

Active Listening

One of the most critical coaching skills, active listening involves fully focusing on the coachee, understanding his/her perspective, and responding thoughtfully. This technique helps to build trust and encourages open communication.

Asking Powerful Questions

Effective coaches ask open-ended questions that prompt reflection and self-discovery. Questions like, "What do you think is the best approach?" or "How would you handle this situation differently?" encourage coachees to think critically and develop their problem-solving skills.

Providing Constructive Feedback

Feedback is essential for growth, but it must be delivered in a way that is both honest and supportive. Effective feedback is specific, focused on behaviour (not personality), and offers clear suggestions for improvement.

Setting SMART Goals

Coaches should help coachees set goals that are Specific, Measurable, Achievable, Relevant, and Time-bound. SMART goals provide clarity and direction, making it easier for coachees to track their progress and stay motivated.

Encouraging Self-Reflection

Regular self-reflection helps coachees gain insight into their strengths and areas for improvement. Coaches can facilitate this process by asking reflective questions and encouraging coachees to keep a journal or log of their experiences.

D. Building a Mentorship Program

Establishing a formal mentorship program within an organization requires careful planning and execution. Here are the key steps involved in building a successful mentorship program:

Define the Program's Objectives

Clearly outline what the mentorship program is intended to achieve. Whether the goal is to accelerate leadership development, improve employee retention, or foster a culture of continuous learning, having well-defined objectives will guide the design and implementation of the program.

Identify Potential Mentors and Mentees

Select mentors who have the experience, knowledge, and interpersonal skills to effectively guide others. Similarly, identify mentees who are motivated and open to learning. It's important to ensure that the mentor-mentee pairs are well-matched in terms of personality, goals, and work styles.

Develop a Mentorship Framework

Create a structure for the mentorship relationship, including the frequency of meetings, the duration of the mentorship, and the topics to be covered. Providing guidelines and resources will help both mentors and mentees get the most out of the relationship.

Provide Training and Support

Offer training for mentors to enhance their mentoring skills and provide them with tools and resources to support their mentees effectively. Regular check-ins and support from the program coordinators can also help address any challenges that arise.

Measure and Evaluate the Program's Effectiveness

Establish metrics to assess the success of the mentorship program. This could include feedback from participants, tracking the achievement of specific goals, or measuring improvements in key performance indicators. Regularly evaluating the program will help to identify areas for improvement and ensure that it continues to meet the needs of the organization.

E. Case Study

David Patel, a Senior Manager at TechSolutions, is renowned within the company for his exceptional mentoring and coaching skills. When the company initiated a leadership development program to identify and nurture future leaders, David was asked to mentor several high-potential employees. Recognizing the diverse talents and aspirations of his mentees, David tailored his approach to meet their individual needs, combining structured guidance with personalized coaching.

One of his mentees, Jessica, was a talented engineer with aspirations of moving into management but lacked confidence in her leadership abilities. David worked closely with Jessica, helping her to identify her strengths and areas for development. He provided her with challenging assignments that stretched her capabilities and offered regular feedback that was both constructive and encouraging. Through their sessions, David also introduced Jessica to key leadership concepts and shared his own experiences, offering insights that textbooks couldn't provide.

As a result of David's mentoring, Jessica grew in confidence and skill, eventually securing a managerial role within the company. David's commitment to her growth didn't stop there; he continued to coach her as she transitioned into her new position, helping her navigate challenges and build her leadership style. Jessica's success, along with that of many others David has mentored, is a testament to the power of effective mentoring and coaching in developing future leaders. David's approach not only empowered his mentees but also contributed to a culture of continuous learning and development at TechSolutions.

F. Conclusion

Mentorship and coaching are powerful tools for developing leadership talent and fostering a culture of growth within an organization. By investing in these practices, leaders can ensure that their teams are not only capable of meeting today's challenges but are also well-prepared for the future. Whether through formal mentorship programs or individual coaching relationships, the impact of these efforts can be profound, leading to increased engagement, improved performance, and a stronger, more resilient organization. As you continue your leadership journey, remember that your role as a mentor or coach is not just to lead, but to inspire others to lead as well.

CHAPTER 14

LEADERSHIP AND
TRAINING PROGRAMS

"The beautiful thing about learning is that nobody can take it away from you." — B.B. King

"Anyone who stops learning is old, whether at twenty or eighty. Anyone who keeps learning stays young." — Henry Ford

A. Introduction

Leadership training programs are essential for equipping current and future leaders with the skills, knowledge, and mindset necessary to navigate the complexities of the modern business environment. These programs serve as a critical investment in the long-term success of an organization, ensuring that leaders at all levels are prepared to guide their teams toward achieving strategic objectives. In this chapter, we will explore the key elements of designing effective leadership training programs, the importance of evaluating their success, and the role of continuous improvement in maintaining the relevance and impact of these initiatives. We will also examine a case scenario that illustrates the practical application of these principles.

B. Designing Effective Training

Designing a leadership training program requires a strategic approach that aligns the training with the organization's goals and the specific needs of its leaders. The following steps are crucial in creating an effective leadership training program:

Identify Training Objectives

Begin by clearly defining the goals of the training program. Are you aiming to develop specific leadership competencies, such as strategic thinking or decision-making? Or is the focus on fostering a particular leadership style that aligns with the organization's culture? Having clear objectives will guide the content and structure of the program.

Assess Leadership Needs

Conduct a thorough needs assessment to determine the skills and knowledge gaps among your leaders. This can be done through surveys, interviews, and performance evaluations. Understanding these gaps will help tailor the training content to address the specific areas where development is needed.

Develop a Customized Curriculum

Based on the training objectives and needs assessment, design a curriculum that is relevant and practical. The curriculum should include a mix of theoretical concepts, practical exercises, case studies, and real-world scenarios. Incorporating diverse training methods, such as workshops, seminars, e-learning modules, and peer-to-peer learning, can enhance the learning experience.

Engage Experienced Trainers

The effectiveness of a leadership training program is heavily influenced by the quality of the trainers. Engage experienced trainers who not only possess deep subject matter expertise but also have the ability to inspire and engage participants. Trainers should be able to relate the training content to real-world challenges and provide actionable insights.

Integrate Real-World Application

Leadership training should not be confined to the classroom. Incorporate opportunities for participants to apply what they have learned in real-world situations. This could include project-based learning, on-the-job assignments, or simulations. Real-world application helps to reinforce learning and ensures that participants can translate theory into practice.

C. Evaluating Program Success

Evaluating the success of a leadership training program is crucial to ensure that it delivers the intended outcomes and provides value to the organization. Here are key steps in the evaluation process:

Set Clear Metrics

Before the training program begins, establish clear metrics for success. These could include improvements in leadership competencies, changes in team performance, or the achievement of specific business outcomes. Having measurable goals allows for a more objective assessment of the program's impact.

Collect Feedback

Gather feedback from participants, trainers, and other stakeholders to assess the program's effectiveness. This feedback can be collected through surveys, focus groups, and interviews. Pay close attention to both qualitative and quantitative data, as both provide valuable insights.

Measure Behavioural Change

One of the most important indicators of a successful leadership training program is the extent to which participants demonstrate behavioural change. This can be measured through performance evaluations, 360-degree feedback, or observing changes in team dynamics and decision-making processes.

Analyze Business Impact

Ultimately, the success of a leadership training program should be reflected in business outcomes. Analyze the impact of the training on key performance indicators such as employee engagement, productivity, and overall business performance. This analysis helps to determine the return on investment (ROI) of the training program.

D. Continuous Improvement

Leadership training is not a one-time event but an ongoing process that requires continuous improvement. To ensure that your training programs remain relevant and effective, consider the following approaches:

Regularly Update Content

Leadership trends and organizational needs evolve over time. Regularly review and update the training content to ensure that it reflects the latest best practices, industry developments, and organizational priorities.

Incorporate Feedback

Use the feedback collected from participants and stakeholders to make adjustments to the training program. Continuous feedback loops help to identify areas for improvement and ensure that the program remains aligned with participants' needs.

Encourage Lifelong Learning

Promote a culture of continuous learning within the organization. Encourage leaders to engage in ongoing professional development, attend external training sessions, and participate in peer learning groups. This not only enhances individual growth but also contributes to the overall development of the organization's leadership capabilities.

Monitor Long-Term Outcomes

Leadership training should have a lasting impact on both the individual participants and the organization as a whole. Monitor the long-term outcomes of the training by tracking participants' career progression, their contributions to the organization, and the overall improvement in leadership quality.

Case Scenario: The Leadership Excellence Initiative at TechSol Inc.

TechSol Inc., a rapidly growing technology company, recognized the need to strengthen its leadership pipeline to support its expansion. The company launched the "Leadership Excellence Initiative," a comprehensive training program designed to develop high-potential employees into effective leaders.

Designing the Program: The program began with a thorough needs assessment, revealing that the company needed leaders who could manage cross-functional teams, drive innovation, and navigate the complexities of a global market. Based on this assessment, the program was designed with a curriculum that included modules on strategic thinking, innovation management, and cross-cultural leadership.

Implementation: The program was delivered through a combination of in-person workshops, online courses, and project-based learning. Participants were assigned real-world projects that required them to apply the concepts they learned in the training. Experienced leaders within the company served as mentors, providing guidance and feedback throughout the program.

Evaluation: The success of the program was evaluated using a multi-tiered approach. Participants' leadership competencies were assessed before and after the program, with significant improvements noted in areas such as strategic thinking and team management. Feedback from participants highlighted the value of the real-world projects and the mentorship component. The program's impact on the business was evident in the improved performance of the teams led by the program graduates, as well as in the successful execution of key strategic initiatives.

Continuous Improvement: Based on the feedback and evaluation results, TechSol Inc. made several adjustments to the program, including adding new modules on digital leadership and enhancing the mentorship process. The company also introduced a follow-up program to provide ongoing support for graduates as they transitioned into leadership roles.

The Leadership Excellence Initiative at TechSol Inc. illustrates the importance of a well-designed, evaluated, and continuously improved leadership training program. By aligning the training with organizational goals and providing participants with practical, real-world experiences, TechSol was able to build a strong leadership pipeline that supported its growth and success.

E. Conclusion

Leadership training programs are a cornerstone of organizational success, providing leaders with the tools and skills they need to guide their teams effectively. By carefully designing these programs, evaluating their outcomes, and committing to continuous improvement, organizations can ensure that their leaders are prepared to meet the challenges of today and tomorrow. As we conclude this exploration of leadership training, remember that the journey of leadership development is ongoing, and the investment in training is one that pays dividends in the form of a resilient, agile, and high-performing organization.

PART VI

A LOOK TOWARDS THE FUTURE

CHAPTER 15

SUCCESSION PLANNING

"Succession planning often results in the selection of
a weaker representation of yourself." — Peter F. Drucker

A. Introduction

Succession planning is a critical aspect of leadership that ensures the long-term stability and continuity of an organization. It involves identifying and developing future leaders who can step into key roles when the current leaders retire, move on, or are otherwise unable to continue in their positions. Succession planning is not just about filling vacancies; it's about preparing the next generation of leaders to carry forward the organization's mission, vision, and values.

B. The Importance of Succession Planning

Succession planning is essential for several reasons. First, it ensures business continuity by minimizing disruptions when leadership transitions occur. Without a well-thought-out succession plan, organizations risk losing valuable knowledge, skills, and leadership momentum. Second, it helps to identify and retain top talent by providing clear career paths and development opportunities. Employees who see a future within the organization are more likely to stay and invest in their growth. Finally, succession planning fosters a culture of leadership development, where preparing for the future is an ongoing priority rather than a reactive process.

C. Steps in Succession Planning

Assessing Organizational Needs

The first step in succession planning is to assess the organization's current and future leadership needs. This involves identifying key roles that are critical to the organization's success and understanding the skills and competencies required for those roles.

Identifying Potential Leaders

Once the critical roles have been identified, the next step is to identify potential successors within the organization. This requires a deep understanding of employees' strengths, career aspirations, and development needs. Tools such as performance evaluations, 360-degree feedback, and talent assessments can be helpful in this process.

Developing Future Leaders

After identifying potential successors, the focus shifts to their development. This involves creating individualized development plans that include training, mentorship, and stretch assignments to build the necessary skills and experience. Providing opportunities for high-potential employees to take on leadership roles, even on a temporary basis, can also accelerate their readiness for future roles.

Monitoring Progress

Succession planning is an ongoing process that requires regular review and adjustment. Leaders should monitor the progress of potential successors, provide feedback, and adjust development plans as needed. Regularly revisiting the succession plan ensures that it remains aligned with the organization's evolving needs.

Implementing the Plan

When a leadership transition becomes imminent, the succession plan is put into action. This involves making a smooth and well-communicated transition, ensuring that the incoming leader is fully prepared to take on his or her new role. The outgoing leader can play a crucial role in mentoring and supporting the successor during this transition period.

D. Challenges in Succession Planning

Succession planning is not without its challenges. One of the most common obstacles is resistance to change, both from potential successors and from existing leaders who may be reluctant to relinquish control. Additionally, organizations may struggle with a lack of diversity in their leadership pipelines, leading to a narrow pool of potential successors. To overcome these challenges, organizations must foster a culture of openness, inclusivity, and continuous development.

Case Study

Karen Thompson, the CEO of HealthFirst Systems, a leading healthcare provider, understood that effective succession planning was crucial to ensuring the long-term stability and success of the organization. With several key executives nearing retirement, Karen took proactive steps to create a comprehensive succession plan that would not only fill these upcoming vacancies but also prepare the organization for future challenges.

Karen began by conducting a thorough assessment of the organization's leadership needs, identifying critical roles that would require strong successors. She then worked closely with the HR department to identify high-potential employees who could be developed for these roles. Karen believed in a holistic approach to leadership development, so she implemented a structured program that included mentoring, leadership training, and cross-functional assignments to broaden the experience of these potential successors.

One of the most successful outcomes of the succession plan was the development of Emily Nguyen, a talented director within the company. Recognizing Emily's potential, Karen personally mentored her, providing guidance and opportunities to lead high-impact projects. Emily was also given the chance to participate in executive-level meetings and decision-making processes, which further prepared her for a senior leadership role.

When the time came for the Chief Operating Officer to retire, Emily was ready to step into the position. Thanks to the comprehensive succession planning process, the transition was smooth, and HealthFirst Systems continued to thrive under Emily's leadership. Karen's foresight in planning for the future ensured that the organization remained strong and capable, even as key leadership roles changed hands. This case study highlights the importance of succession planning in maintaining organizational continuity and developing the next generation of leaders.

E. Conclusion

Succession planning is a vital component of sustainable leadership. By proactively identifying and developing future leaders, organizations can ensure their continued success and resilience in the face of change. Effective succession planning requires a strategic approach, a commitment to leadership development, and a willingness to embrace the future with confidence. By investing in the next generation of leaders, organizations not only secure their future but also create a legacy of strong, capable leadership.

CHAPTER 16

A LOOK AT LEADERSHIP
IN THE FUTURE

*"Leaders establish the vision for the future and set
the strategy for getting there."*- John P. Kotter

"The best way to predict the future is to invent it." - *Alan Kay*

A. Introduction

As we look towards the future, it's clear that the landscape of leadership is evolving. Rapid technological advancements, shifting societal values, and an increasingly interconnected global economy are reshaping the way leaders think, act, and guide their organizations. This chapter explores the emerging trends and challenges that will define leadership in the future, and how current and aspiring leaders can prepare for this new era.

B. Emerging Trends in Leadership

Technological Integration

Technology is transforming every aspect of business, and leadership is no exception. The future of leadership will require a deep understanding of digital tools, data analytics, and artificial intelligence. Leaders will need to leverage technology not only to improve efficiency and decision-making but also to innovate and create new opportunities.

Globalization and Diversity

As the world becomes more interconnected, leaders will need to navigate the complexities of global markets and diverse workforces. This will require cultural competence, adaptability, and the ability to manage teams across different geographies and time zones. Embracing diversity will also be crucial, as diverse teams bring a wide range of perspectives and ideas that drive innovation.

Sustainability and Corporate Responsibility:

Future leaders will be expected to prioritize sustainability and ethical practices. As consumers and employees alike demand greater corporate responsibility, leaders will need to balance profit with purpose. This involves making decisions that consider environmental, social, and governance (ESG) factors and leading organizations in a way that contributes positively to society.

Agility and Resilience

The pace of change is accelerating, and future leaders must be agile and resilient in the face of uncertainty. This means being able to pivot quickly in response to new challenges, embrace change, and lead their teams through ambiguity. Leaders will need to foster a culture of continuous learning and adaptability within their organizations.

Human-Centered Leadership

Despite the rise of technology, the future of leadership will remain deeply human. Leaders will need to emphasize empathy, emotional intelligence, and relationship-building. As the nature of work evolves, with remote and hybrid models becoming more common, leaders will need to find new ways to connect with and motivate their teams, ensuring that people feel valued and engaged.

C. Preparing for the Future of Leadership

To thrive in the future, leaders must begin preparing today. This involves:

Continuous Learning

Leaders should commit to lifelong learning, and staying informed about new technologies, industry trends, and leadership practices. This may involve formal education, attending conferences, and engaging with thought leaders in the field.

Building a Diverse Network

A strong, diverse network is invaluable for navigating the complexities of the future. Leaders should seek out relationships with people from different backgrounds, industries, and perspectives to broaden their understanding and approach to leadership.

Embracing Innovation

Future leaders must be willing to experiment, take risks, and embrace new ideas. This requires a mindset that values innovation and creativity, and the ability to create a culture where these qualities are nurtured.

Fostering a Culture of Inclusion

As diversity becomes increasingly important, leaders must create inclusive environments where all stakeholders feel they belong and can contribute their best work. This involves not only promoting diversity in hiring but also ensuring that all voices are heard and valued.

D. Challenges of Future Leadership

The future of leadership is not without its challenges. Leaders will need to navigate the ethical implications of new technologies, manage the tensions between globalization and local interests, and address the growing demands for transparency and accountability. Additionally, the pressure to constantly innovate and adapt can lead to burnout if not managed carefully. Leaders must be proactive in addressing these challenges, balancing the demands of the present with the opportunities of the future.

E. Case Study

Alex Rodriguez, the Chief Innovation Officer at FutureTech Enterprises, exemplifies forward-thinking leadership in a rapidly evolving technological landscape. Recognizing the fast pace of change and the increasing importance of digital transformation, Alex spearheaded an initiative to position FutureTech as a leader in emerging technologies such as artificial intelligence, blockchain, and quantum computing.

Understanding that traditional leadership models might not suffice in this new era, Alex adopted a leadership style that emphasized agility, continuous learning, and inclusivity. He fostered a culture of innovation within the company by encouraging cross-disciplinary collaboration and creating an environment where experimentation and calculated risk-taking were not only allowed but celebrated. Alex also placed a strong emphasis on ethical considerations, ensuring that the development and deployment of new technologies aligned with societal values and long-term sustainability.

To prepare the organization for future challenges, Alex implemented a comprehensive leadership development program that focused on equipping the next generation of leaders with the skills needed for the future. This program included immersive experiences in emerging markets, partnerships with leading tech universities, and mentorship opportunities with industry pioneers. Alex also embraced remote work and digital collaboration tools, recognizing that the future of work would be more flexible and global.

Under Alex's leadership, FutureTech not only stayed ahead of industry trends but also set new standards in innovation and ethical leadership. The company's proactive approach to embracing the future, coupled with Alex's commitment to developing future leaders, ensured that FutureTech remained at the forefront of the technology industry. This case study highlights the qualities and strategies that will define successful leadership in the future, demonstrating the importance of adaptability, continuous learning, and a forward-looking vision.

F. Conclusion

The future of leadership promises to be both exciting and challenging. As the world continues to change at an unprecedented pace, leaders must be prepared to evolve alongside it. By embracing technology, prioritizing diversity and inclusion, and maintaining a human-centered approach, leaders can guide their organizations to success in this new era. The future of leadership is about more than just managing change—it's about leading with vision, purpose, and a commitment to making a positive impact on the world. As we look ahead, the leaders who will thrive are those who are not only prepared for the future but are actively shaping it.

CONCLUSION

A. The Ongoing Journey of Leadership

Leadership is a journey that never truly ends; it is a continuous process of growth, learning, and self-discovery. Throughout this book, we have explored the multifaceted nature of leadership, delving into the skills, attributes, and strategies that define successful leaders. However, the essence of leadership lies not in mastering these concepts once, but in revisiting and refining them throughout your career.

The journey of leadership is characterized by a deep commitment to personal and professional development. It requires leaders to remain curious, open to new ideas, and willing to challenge their assumptions. True leadership is about embracing change—not just reacting to it, but actively seeking it out as a means of growth. It is about being resilient in the face of adversity and using every challenge as an opportunity to become a better leader.

Moreover, leadership is an inherently relational endeavour. It is about building and nurturing relationships, earning trust, and empowering others to achieve their potential. As you continue on your leadership journey, it is crucial to remember that your success is intertwined with the success of those you lead. Cultivate empathy, listen actively, and remain attuned to the needs and aspirations of your team. By doing so, you will not only enhance your own leadership but also contribute to the growth and success of those around you.

Leadership is not a solitary path; it is one that is enriched by the insights and experiences of others. Engage with mentors, peers, and colleagues who can offer diverse perspectives and challenge you to think differently. Surround yourself with individuals who inspire you to strive for excellence and who hold you accountable to your highest standards.

Finally, the journey of leadership is deeply personal. It is about aligning your leadership style with your core values and principles. It is about leading with authenticity and integrity, and ensuring that your actions consistently reflect the kind of leader you aspire to be. As you continue to evolve as a leader, take the time to reflect on your journey—celebrate your successes, learn from your setbacks, and remain steadfast in your commitment to continuous improvement.

B. Staying Ahead in a Dynamic World

The world in which we live is characterized by constant change and unpredictability. In such a dynamic environment, the role of a leader is not just to respond to change but to anticipate it, shape it, and guide the organization through it. Staying ahead in a dynamic world requires a proactive mindset, one that is always looking forward and ready to adapt to new challenges and opportunities.

To remain effective in this rapidly evolving landscape, leaders must embrace agility as a core competency. Agility in leadership means being able to pivot quickly in response to shifting market conditions, technological advancements, or unexpected disruptions. It requires leaders to be flexible in their thinking and decision-making, willing to explore new approaches, and unafraid to take calculated risks. In a world where change is the only constant, the ability to adapt swiftly and effectively is what sets successful leaders apart.

Innovation is another critical component of staying ahead. Leaders must foster a culture of innovation within their organizations, encouraging creativity, experimentation, and the pursuit of new ideas. This involves not only supporting innovation at the strategic level but also empowering individuals at all levels of the organization to contribute to the innovation process. By creating an environment where innovation thrives, leaders can ensure that their organizations remain competitive and relevant in an ever-changing market.

In addition to agility and innovation, leaders must also prioritize continuous learning. The knowledge and skills that are relevant today may become obsolete tomorrow, and staying ahead requires a commitment to lifelong learning. This means not only keeping up with industry trends and developments but also seeking out new knowledge and experiences that can broaden your perspective and enhance your leadership capabilities. Engage in ongoing professional development, attend conferences, participate in workshops, and seek out opportunities to learn from others—whether they are peers, mentors, or even those you lead.

Furthermore, staying ahead in a dynamic world requires a global mindset. In an increasingly interconnected world, leaders must be attuned to the global forces that influence their industry and organization. This involves understanding cultural differences, being aware of global market trends, and being able to navigate the complexities of leading diverse teams. Leaders who possess a global mindset are better equipped to seize opportunities and address challenges that arise from the global nature of today's business environment.

Finally, as you navigate the complexities of a dynamic world, remember that leadership is as much about guiding others as it is about setting the course for the future. Your ability to inspire and mobilize your team will be crucial in steering your organization through change. Communicate your vision clearly, foster a sense of shared purpose, and lead by example. By doing so, you will not only stay ahead of the curve but also empower your team to achieve extraordinary results in the face of uncertainty.

In conclusion, the journey of leadership is one of constant evolution, shaped by the challenges we face and the lessons we learn along the way. It requires a commitment to continuous improvement, an ability to adapt to change, and a deep understanding of the dynamic world in which we operate. As you move forward, let the insights and principles explored in this book serve as your global positioning system (GPS), guiding you to lead with confidence, purpose, and a relentless drive to excel. The future is uncertain, but with the right mindset and tools, you can navigate it with courage and foresight, leading your organization to success and leaving a lasting impact on those you lead.

SUMMARY OF CHAPTERS

W̲e have decided to place this Summary of Chapters at the end of the book as a recap, reinforcing the key takeaways and giving you, the readers, a clear sense of the overall message of **The Leadership GPS.** We hope this placement will be particularly effective for reinforcing learning and ensuring that the main concepts are retained.

This summary encapsulates the key themes and insights from each chapter of *The Leadership GPS*, offering a comprehensive overview of the essential skills and strategies required for effective leadership in today's dynamic world.

Chapter 1: Defining Leadership

This chapter lays the groundwork by exploring what leadership truly means. It discusses the various definitions of leadership, distinguishing between management and leadership, and identifying the qualities that make someone an effective leader. The chapter also introduces the concept of leadership as both an art and a science, setting the stage for a deeper exploration of leadership principles.

Chapter 2: Core Leadership Principles

Core principles such as integrity, accountability, and vision are the bedrock of effective leadership. This chapter delves into these fundamental principles, explaining how they guide decision-making, build trust, and foster a positive organizational culture. Practical examples illustrate how these principles manifest in everyday leadership scenarios.

Chapter 3: Self-awareness and Personal Growth

Self-awareness is crucial for personal and professional development. This chapter emphasizes the importance of understanding one's strengths, weaknesses, values, and motivations. It also explores tools and techniques for self-assessment, and how personal growth contributes to becoming a more effective and authentic leader.

Chapter 4: Building a Strong Team

Effective leadership is as much about building strong teams as it is about leading individuals. This chapter discusses strategies for assembling diverse teams, fostering collaboration, and creating an environment where every team member can thrive. It also covers team dynamics, trust-building, and the importance of a shared vision.

Chapter 5: Effective Communication

Communication is the lifeblood of leadership. This chapter explores the different facets of communication, including active listening, clear messaging, and non-verbal cues. It offers practical tips for improving communication skills and highlights the role of communication in conflict resolution, motivation, and team alignment.

Chapter 6: Motivation and Empowerment

Motivating and empowering others is a key responsibility of a leader. This chapter examines various motivational theories and practical strategies for inspiring teams. It also discusses the importance of empowerment, showing how leaders can delegate authority and foster an environment where employees feel valued and motivated to perform at their best.

Chapter 7: Change Management

Change is inevitable, and effective leaders must be able to manage it successfully. This chapter provides a framework for leading change, from planning and communication to execution and follow-up. It discusses the emotional aspects of change, the importance of stakeholder engagement, and strategies for overcoming resistance.

Chapter 8: Conflict Resolution

Conflict is a natural part of any organizational setting, but it can be managed constructively. This chapter explores the sources of conflict, different conflict resolution styles, and techniques for resolving disputes in a way that strengthens relationships and enhances team performance. The focus is on turning conflicts into opportunities for growth and improvement.

Chapter 9: Crisis Management

Crisis situations test the mettle of a leader. This chapter offers insights into the principles of effective crisis management, including preparation, quick decision-making, and clear communication. It discusses how leaders can maintain calm under pressure, make informed decisions in uncertain situations, and lead their teams through crises with resilience and confidence.

Chapter 10: Visionary Leadership

Visionary leadership is about seeing the big picture and inspiring others to work towards it. This chapter explores how to develop and communicate a compelling vision that aligns with organizational goals and motivates teams. It also discusses the importance of strategic thinking and long-term planning in achieving that vision.

Chapter 11: Innovation and Creativity

Innovation and creativity are vital for organizational growth and sustainability. This chapter focuses on how leaders can foster a culture of creativity within their teams, encouraging experimentation and the free exchange of ideas. It covers strategies for managing innovation, including supporting risk-taking and ensuring that creative ideas are aligned with business objectives.

Chapter 12: Decision-making and Problem-Solving

Effective leaders are decisive and adept at solving problems. This chapter provides a systematic approach to decision-making, balancing analytical thinking with intuition. It covers problem-solving techniques, the role of data in decision-making, and the importance of involving the right people in the process to make informed and effective decisions.

Chapter 13: Mentorship and Coaching

Mentorship and coaching are essential for developing future leaders. This chapter explores the roles of mentors and coaches, providing guidance on how to nurture talent, offer constructive feedback, and foster a growth mindset. It also discusses the benefits of creating a structured mentorship program within the organization.

Chapter 14: Leadership Training Programs

Leadership training programs are crucial for ongoing leadership development. This final chapter offers a comprehensive guide to designing and implementing effective training programs. It discusses how to align training with organizational goals, evaluate their success, and continuously improve the programs to meet evolving needs. A case scenario illustrates the practical application of these concepts.

Chapter 15: Succession Planning

In this chapter, the focus is on the crucial process of succession planning, which ensures the continuity and long-term success of an organization by preparing future leaders. The chapter discusses the importance of identifying key leadership roles and developing potential successors within the organization. It outlines the steps involved in succession planning, including assessing organizational needs, identifying potential leaders, and creating individualized development plans. The chapter also highlights the challenges that organizations may face in succession planning, such as resistance to change and lack of diversity, and provides strategies for overcoming these obstacles. Ultimately, the chapter emphasizes that effective succession planning is an ongoing process that prepares organizations for seamless leadership transitions, ensuring sustained growth and stability.

Chapter 16: A Look at Leadership in the Future

This chapter explores the evolving landscape of leadership and the trends that will shape its future. It examines the impact of technological integration, globalization, and diversity on leadership roles, emphasizing the need for leaders to adapt to these changes. The chapter also discusses the increasing importance of sustainability and corporate responsibility, highlighting the role of ethical leadership in future organizations. Additionally, it emphasizes the need for agility, resilience, and human-centered leadership in a rapidly changing world. The chapter provides guidance on how current and aspiring leaders can prepare for the future by embracing continuous learning, building diverse networks, fostering innovation, and creating inclusive cultures. The chapter concludes by acknowledging the challenges of future leadership but encourages leaders to actively shape the future with vision, purpose, and a commitment to making a positive impact.

APPENDICES

TOOLS AND RESOURCES
FOR LEADERS

In this section, you'll find a curated list of tools and resources that can enhance your leadership capabilities and support the implementation of the strategies discussed in this book. These tools are designed to help you manage teams, develop leadership skills, and navigate the complexities of modern organizational dynamics.

Leadership Assessment Tools

Myers-Briggs Type Indicator (MBTI): A widely used personality assessment that helps leaders understand their own and their team members' personality types, improving communication and collaboration.

360-Degree Feedback Surveys: Tools like Qualtrics or SurveyMonkey offer customizable 360-degree feedback surveys to gather comprehensive insights from peers, subordinates, and supervisors about your leadership performance.

Emotional Intelligence (EQ) Assessments: Tools like the EQ-i 2.0 assess your emotional intelligence, providing insights into your ability to recognize and manage emotions in yourself and others.

Team Management Tools

Trello/Asana: Project management tools that help you organize tasks, assign responsibilities, and track progress, fostering efficient team collaboration.

Slack/Microsoft Teams: Communication platforms that streamline team interactions, enabling real-time messaging, file sharing, and video conferencing to keep everyone aligned.

Google Workspace: A suite of productivity tools (Docs, Sheets, Slides) that supports collaborative work, document sharing, and efficient management of team projects.

Leadership Development Platforms

LinkedIn Learning: Offers a vast library of leadership courses on topics ranging from communication and management to strategic thinking and emotional intelligence.

Coursera/edX: Online platforms offering leadership courses from top universities and institutions, covering a wide range of topics including negotiation, decision-making, and leadership in a global context.

Harvard Business Review (HBR): A valuable resource for articles, case studies, and insights on leadership, management, and organizational behaviour.

Coaching and Mentoring Resources

MentorcliQ: A software platform designed to manage and scale mentoring programs, providing tools for matching mentors and mentees, tracking progress, and measuring outcomes.

BetterUp: A coaching platform that connects leaders with professional coaches to support personal and professional growth through tailored development plans.

Coaching for Performance by Sir John Whitmore: A practical guide for leaders looking to develop their coaching skills, with frameworks and techniques to enhance performance.

(https://www.amazon.com/Coaching-Performance-Fifth-Principles-ANNIVERSARY/dp/1473658128)

RECOMMENDED READING

This list of recommended readings offers additional insights and perspectives on leadership, drawing from a range of disciplines including psychology, management, and organizational theory. These books are selected to deepen your understanding of the concepts covered in "The Leadership GPS" and to inspire further growth on your leadership journey.

1. "The Art of Leadership" by Max De Pree

An exploration of the relationship between leaders and followers, focusing on the importance of integrity, trust, and the human side of leadership. (https://www.amazon.com/Leadership-Art-Max-Depree/dp/B0077EEPTO)

2. "Leaders Eat Last" by Simon Sinek

A compelling look at how great leaders create environments where people feel safe, valued, and empowered, fostering trust and cooperation within organizations. (https://simonsinek.com/books/leaders-eat-last/)

3. "Emotional Intelligence" by Daniel Goleman

A groundbreaking book that explains why emotional intelligence (EQ) is as important as IQ for effective leadership, with practical

advice on developing your own EQ.
(https://www.amazon.com/Emotional-Intelligence-Matter-More-Than/dp/055338371X)

4. "The Innovator's Dilemma" by Clayton M. Christensen

This book explores the challenges of sustaining innovation in established organizations, offering insights into how leaders can navigate disruptive technologies and maintain their competitive edge. (https://www.amazon.com/Innovators-Dilemma-Revolutionary-Change-Business/dp/0062060244)

5. "Good to Great" by Jim Collins

An analysis of what makes companies transition from good to great, with key insights into the leadership qualities that drive sustainable success. (https://www.amazon.com/Good-Great-Some-Companies-Others/dp/0066620996)

6. "Drive: The Surprising Truth About What Motivates Us" by Daniel H. Pink

A deep dive into the psychology of motivation, offering practical advice for leaders on how to create environments that tap into intrinsic motivation to drive performance. (https://www.amazon.com/Drive-Surprising-Truth-About-Motivates/dp/1594484805)

7. "Start with Why" by Simon Sinek

A book that challenges leaders to inspire action by starting with the 'why'—the purpose, cause, or belief that drives an organization. (https://simonsinek.com/books/start-with-why/)

8. "The Five Dysfunctions of a Team" by Patrick Lencioni

A leadership fable that highlights the common pitfalls that can derail teams, with actionable strategies for building trust, fostering accountability, and achieving results.
(https://www.amazon.com/Five-Dysfunctions-Team-Leadership-Fable/dp/0787960756)

9. "Crucial Conversations: Tools for Talking When Stakes Are High" by Kerry Patterson, Joseph Grenny, Ron McMillan, and Al Switzler

A guide to handling difficult conversations with skill and confidence, offering techniques for effective communication in high-pressure situations. (https://www.amazon.com/Crucial-Conversations-Talking-Stakes-Second/dp/0071771328)

10. "The Leadership Challenge" by James M. Kouzes and Barry Z. Posner

A comprehensive book on leadership that presents research-based practices for leaders to engage and inspire their teams. (https://www.goodreads.com/book/show/1758199.The_Leadership _Challenge)

These books provide valuable resources for leaders at all stages of their journey, offering the knowledge and skills necessary to navigate the challenges of leadership with confidence and competence.

GLOSSARY

This glossary provides definitions and explanations of specialized or unfamiliar terms used in leadership discussions and discourses. It helps readers better understand key concepts and terminology, making the content more accessible and enhancing their overall comprehension of the material.

A

Accountability
Members of an organization who are given responsibility and authority are held accountable for the results.

Achievement motive
Motivation to seek high performance and success.

Acquiescent response set
Agreement with statements, regardless of their content.

Action research
Research whose objective includes the implemented solution of the research problem using the diagnosis of the problem, the collection of data, and the analysis and feedback of data.

Adaptation level
An individual's expectations and experience set a standard against which events or objects are perceived.

Ad hoc group
A temporary group established to deal with a problem or problems (also Task force).

Affect (noun)
Feeling; emotional reaction.

Affiliation motive (nAff)
The motivation to belong and to be with other people.

Affirmative action
Positive programs to increase opportunities for the employment and promotion of members of disadvantaged groups.

Algorithm
A procedure used to solve a set of problems by an explicit formula.

Alienation
A generalized sense of meaninglessness, helplessness, and social isolation that contributes to the disinhibition of personal controls against engaging in deviant behaviour.

Altruism
Helping others with no obvious benefit to oneself and with few expectations for personal gain.

Analog
A physical, mechanical, or electrical model of an object or concept about which measurements and calculations can be made.

Anomie
The reduced social control against deviant behaviour that is due to a disregard for norms and standards.

Anxiety
Generalized, diffuse apprehension.

A posteriori
Explanations are offered after the facts are known.

A priori
Hypotheses are formulated before the facts are known.

Arbitration
A situation in which a third party renders a decision for two parties who are in conflict.

Artifact
The results of an arbitrary method, rather than the true state of affairs.

Artificial intelligence (AI)
The emulation of the problem-solving, linguistic, and other capabilities of human beings by means of a computer.

Assumed similarity
We assume that we are like other people in values, interests, beliefs, and personality (see Projection).

Attenuation
Reduction from a theoretically true correlation because of the unreliability of one or both measures correlated.

Attitude
An affective, evaluative, relatively enduring reaction, positive or negative, toward an object or proposition.

Attribution theory
A theory of the way people impute intentions to other persons or situations.

Auditing
Verification of the validity of data, statements, and records.

Autonomy

The degree of freedom in carrying out an assignment.

Aversive reinforcement

Reinforcing conditions that inhibit the reinforced behaviour; also Negative reinforcement.

B

Batch production

The production of quantities of similar items, rather than mixes of items.

Behaviour modification

Changing behaviour by changing the consequences of that behaviour. Desired new behaviour is rewarded (positively reinforced); undesired old behaviour is punished or positive consequences are removed (negatively reinforced).

Behaviour shaping

Behaviour modification in which small increments of behaviour are reinforced in the direction of the desired behaviour until a final desired result is achieved.

Biased sample

A sample that is unrepresentative because of one or more sources of systematic error.

Binary

Involving two digits or states.

Boundary-spanning roles

Liaison roles that connect departments or organizations with each other and with the environment.

Bounded rationality

Managers make the best decisions they can within the constraints of limited information about possible alternatives and the consequences of the alternatives.

Brainstorming

The generation of ideas without evaluating them; a maximum number of ideas can be generated in a limited time.

Buffering

Actions or events to seal off processes from external variations.

Bureaucracy

An organization that is operated on the basis of rules, regulations, and orderliness and that focuses on legitimacy, the duties of jobs, and the rights of office. It is characterized by standardization, hierarchical control, specified authority, and responsibilities.

Bureaucratic personality

The preference for rules, regulations, and order in running organizations.

Burnout

Emotional, mental, and physical exhaustion resulting from continuing exposure to stress.

Business game

A simulation of a business operated by two or more players competing with other businesses in a common market.

C

Career plateau

A prolonged halt in promotion up the corporate ladder.

Centralization

The degree of concentration of authority in a central location at the top of the organization.

Chain of command

The hierarchy of authority in an organization from top to bottom. Members are supposed to know to whom they should report and who reports to them.

Change Agent

An individual who guides the process of group or organizational change.

Channel

The communication path along which information flows.

Classical organization theory

Early efforts to identify the principles of effective management.

Code

A system for representing information and rules.

Coefficient alpha

The internal consistency or reliability of a test or measure based on the average intercorrelation among its items.

Cognition

A mental event in which perceptions, memories, beliefs, and thoughts are processed; the sensing of many narrow segmented categories in behaviour or events, rather than a few broad classifications.

Cognitive dissonance

The holding of incompatible beliefs and cognitions.

Cognitive dissonance theory

The theory that it is unpleasant to maintain strongly held beliefs that clash with facts and that people are motivated to resolve the incompatibility by maintaining the beliefs and denying the facts.

Cognitive Framework

The categories and their connections into which individuals place events, behaviours, objects, attributes, and concepts.

Cohesiveness

The forces that hold a group together; the attractiveness of a group for its members and the members for one another.

Collective bargaining

The negotiation and administration of agreements between labour and management about wages, working conditions, benefits, and other labour-management issues.

Commitment

Strong, positive involvement; continuing concern.

Common factor

The statistical representation of a factor underlying two or more variables.

Communality

The sum of squares of factor loadings for a designated variable; the total variance that is due to the factors that this variable shares with all other variables in an intercorrelated set.

Communication overload

The receipt of excessive amounts of information such that the information cannot be processed satisfactorily.

Complexity leadership

Leaders go beyond ordinary management to coordinate the complexities of the organization.

Compliance

Acting that is consistent with rules, norms, or influence by others.

Compression of salaries

Because of changes in labour market conditions, newly hired employees may begin employment at salaries that are near to or the same as those with seniority, more experience, but similar other credentials.

Compulsory arbitration

A negotiation in which the arbiter's decision is binding on the parties in conflict.

Computer-assisted instruction (CAI)

Instruction by computers that substitutes for human instruction.

Concept

A mental image formed from a set of observations; a definition that labels and provides meaning to the observed reality.

Conflict management

Intervening as needed to avoid, reduce, or resolve conflicts.

Confrontation

A situation in which parties in conflict directly face, oppose, and resist each other on the issues.

Connective leadership

Achieving styles (behavioral strategies) to deal with a changing environment.

Consensus

An emotionally and intellectually acceptable group decision.

Content analysis

An objective, systematic, and usually quantitative description of communications as observed, recorded, or documented.

Contingency table

A display of the frequency of individuals or cases, classified according to two or more attributes.

Continuous processing

Inputs of energy and materials are transformed into products in a flow for a period of time, such as occurs in a petrochemical refinery.

Controlling

The process of monitoring and correcting organizational activities to see that they conform to plans.

Co-optation

A situation in which authorities choose their successors, colleagues, and assistants.

Coordination

Integration of the activities of the separate parts of a group or organization.

Correlation coefficient

The relationship between two variables obtained from the same set of cases. It can range from 11.00 through 0.00 to 21.00. It is the ratio of how much one (standardized) variable's changes coincide with the changes in the other (standardized) variable.

Counterculture

A culture that is radically divergent from the mainstream culture of the society of which it is a part.

Covariance

The mean of the products of the deviations of each of two variables from its own mean.

Criterion

A standard of performance; the measure against which other measures are calibrated.

Critical incidents method

A performance appraisal in which the supervisor keeps a record over a period of time of the behaviours of each subordinate that are critical to the performance of the job. Also, a survey method for collecting desired and undesired critical behaviours from a sample of employees.

D

Damage control
Explanations to offset the effects of a leader's failures and mistakes.

Decentralization
The delegation of power and authority from a central, higher authority to lower levels of the organization, which often results in smaller, self-contained organizational units.

Decision making
Identifying and selecting a course of action to solve a problem.

Decode
To convert coded data into readable and meaningful information.

Deep change
The process of radical alteration or transformation that occurs infrequently and with profound effects on the individual or group.

Deindividuation
A state of being in which an individual in a collection of people does not feel personally identifiable by others.

Dejobbing
An individual worker is assigned to complete a variety of tasks at different times rather than a bundle of the same tasks.

Demand characteristics
Explicit and implicit perceptual cues of what behaviour is expected in a situation.

Departmentalization
The grouping into departments of similar, logically connected work activities.

Dependent variable
A variable whose changes are the consequences of changes in other variables.

Differentiation
Separating and focusing on the differences between individuals, groups, and the activities in an organization.

Division of labour
The breakdown of a complex task into components so that different individuals are responsible for a limited set of more closely connected or similar activities, instead of the task as a whole.

Dogmatism
A close-minded rigid style with beliefs that are authoritarian in content.

Double-loop learning
Errors are corrected, resulting in a change of values about what is important to change; actions are then taken accordingly. In single-loop learning, values remain unchanged and no actions are taken.

Downsizing
Making smaller.

Dramaturgy
Managing impressions by controlling information or cues to be imparted to others.

E

Efficiency
The use of minimum costs and resources in achieving organizational objectives.

Ego
The part of one's personality that is oriented toward acting reasonably and realistically (see Id and Superego).

Empathy
The internalization of the feelings of another person.

Empirically-oriented leadership
Relies on data and information.

Encoding
The translation of information into a series of symbols for communication.

Equity
The fairness of rewards and punishments; a situation in which the ratio of outcomes to inputs for a person is equal to the same ratio for comparison persons.

Ethicality
Implied standards of morally acceptable conduct with emphasis on moral principles.

Ethnocentrism
The rejection of foreigners, aliens, and outgroups; the extreme favouring of one's own group. Also belief that the home country is superior to other countries and that methods that work at home can be exported elsewhere (see Geocentrism and Polycentrism).

Expectancy
An estimate or judgment of the likelihood that some outcome or event will occur.

Expectancy theory
The theory that an effort to achieve high performance is a function of the perceived likelihood that high performance can be achieved and will be rewarded if achieved and that the reward will be worth the effort that is expended.

Experiment

The manipulation of one or more independent variables and the control of other related variables to observe one or more dependent variables.

Experimental control

The elimination or holding of some variables constant, to examine the effects of other variables that are allowed to vary.

External environment

The environment outside the organization or the independent group.

Extrinsic rewards

Pay, promotion, and fringe benefits, apart from the satisfaction that is derived from the work itself.

F

Factor analysis

A statistical technique to extract the smallest number of underlying factors accounting for a larger set of variables.

Fear of success

The fear that envy and dislike by others will accompany one's success.

Feedback

The receiver's expression of her or his reaction to the sender's message or actions. Also, information about the results of one's behaviour, efforts, or performance that can result in correction and control.

Field experiment

The use of the controlled laboratory method in a real-life setting.

Field study

The examination of the relations and interactions among variables in real-life settings, without the manipulation of variables as in a field experiment.

First impression

One's impression of others that is formed early in a relationship, that often has a lasting impact.

First-line managers

Managers who are at the lowest level in the management hierarchy and who are responsible only for the work of operating employees, not for the work of other managers.

Flexible organization

An organization in which the policies, structure, relationships, and jobs are loosely defined and open to alteration.

Forecasting

The prediction of outcomes and future trends.

Formal authority

Legitimate or position power; the right to exert influence because of one's hierarchical position in the organization.

Formal group

A group that is created by a formal authority and is directed toward achieving specific objectives.

Formalization

A situation in which rules, policies, and procedures in organizations are written and institutionalized (see Bureaucracy).

Functional organization

An organization that is departmentalized so that those engaged in the same functional activity, such as marketing, are grouped into one department.

G

Game theory
The explanation of the behaviour of rational people in competitive and conflict situations.

Gender
Grammatical categories, male, female, and neuter, such as he, she, and it. Commonly misapplied to the two biologically distinct sexes, male and female.

General manager
An individual who is responsible for all departments within a larger division, such as a manufacturing plant.

Geocentrism
A world view of management, operations, and opportunities rather than one limited to a single nation or nationality (Ethnocentrism) or an independent collection of countries (Polycentrism).

Grapevine
The paths through which informal communications are passed in an organization.

Group decision support system (GDSS)
A computerized information system in a group meeting to make better use of information for group decisions.

Groupthink
Faulty processes resulting in group decisions that are poorer than those of the individual members working alone.

H

Habituated followers
Blindly trusting followers of the charismatic or pseudo transformational leader.

Halo effect
The influence of overall impressions on the rating of a specific characteristic.

Hawthorne effect
The performance of employees who receive special attention will be better simply because the employees received that attention.

Hedonism
Motivation that is attained by gaining pleasure and avoiding pain.

Heuristics
"Rule of thumb" solutions to problems that are based on past experience rather than explicit formulas.

Hierarchical organization
In a hierarchical organization, except for the member at the top, each member has a superior; and except for those at the bottom, each member has one or more subordinates.

Hypothesis
A conditional prediction about the relationship among concepts or among variables, often generated from a theory, that is subjected to empirical verification.

I

Id
The part of the personality that is the repository of basic drives and unsocialized impulses, including sex and aggression.

Idealistic leadership

Relies on intuition and a minimum of data and information. Ideologue A convinced advocate of a specific set of doctrines, attitudes, and beliefs.

Ideology

A strongly held set of values, attitudes, and beliefs that explain the world.

Implicit theories

The tendencies of individuals to weave characteristics of others or characteristics of events into explanatory patterns.

Incremental adjustments

Problem-solving in which each successive action represents a small change.

Independent variable

A variable that is manipulated in an experiment whose changes are considered to be the cause of changes in other variables (the dependent variables); variables selected in a survey for the same purpose.

Inflection point

Major change in technology, business, or performance evidenced in a changing trend in a graph.

Informal communication

Communication that is not officially sanctioned (see Grapevine).

Informal group

A group that voluntarily arises from the needs of individuals and the attraction of people to one another because of common values and interests; an unofficial group that is created without the sanction of a higher organizational authority.

Informal organization
The relationships between members of an organization that are based on friendship, propinquity, and personal and social needs.

Ingratiation
An attempt to influence other people by flattering them.

Integration
The joining of elements to work together in a unified way. Internal environment Workers, managers, technology, working conditions, and the culture in the organization.

Internalized
Behaviour, compliance, and conformity are consistent with one's beliefs and values.

Internal locus of control
The belief that the rewards one receives result from one's own efforts, rather than because of chance or the effects of others.

Interpretive strategy
Attention placed on perceptions, feelings, values, symbols, and nuances rather than simple realities.

J,K

Job
A collection of tasks grouped together similarly in a number of similar positions in a given organization.

Job enlargement
The combining of various operations at a similar level into one job to provide more variety for workers.

Job enrichment
Providing a job with more challenge, meaning, autonomy, and responsibility.

Job satisfaction
Attitudes and feelings about one's job.

Job scope
The number of separate operations a particular job requires before a cycle is repeated.

Job specialization
The division of work into standardized, simplified tasks.

Job specification
A description of the skills and abilities necessary to perform a particular job.

L

Lame duck
A leader whose power has declined because his or her tenure in the leadership position is near its end.

Lateral (or horizontal) communication
Communication between departments of an organization that generally follows the workflow, thus providing a direct channel for coordination and problem-solving.

Leader-member exchange (LMX)
Interaction of a leader with an individual member of the group or the average member of the group in contrast to the interaction of a leader with the group of members.

Learned helplessness
A condition in which persons become passive, depressed, and unable to learn to cope with the situation.

Likert scale
A scale in which respondents are asked to indicate how much they agree or disagree with an attitudinal statement.

Linear programming

A method for the optimal allocation of limited resources to attain a goal.

Line personnel

Those managers and workers who are directly responsible for achieving organizational goals (in contrast to staff personnel, who provide support services for the line personnel).

LMX

See Leader-member exchange.

Locus of control

The degree to which individuals are controlled by their internal motives, habits, and values, rather than by external forces.

Logic

Principles and criteria of validity in thought and demonstration; the application of truth tables, the relations of propositions, and the consistency of deductions and assumptions.

M

Management by objectives (MBO)

A formal set of procedures to review the progress toward common goals of organizational superiors and their immediate subordinates.

Management information system (MIS)

A formal, usually computerized, system to provide management with information.

Manipulation

An attempt to influence others in which the manipulator tries to conceal the effort from the target of the influence.

Marginality
The position of people at the boundary between two societies, who are often uncertain about their identity and status.

Mathematical model
A facsimile of reality in mathematical terms; a description of a process and parameters and their relationships to one another and to environments.

Matriarchal
A female-dominated family or society in which the woman (wife or mother) is most influential.

Matrix organization
An organization in which each subordinate reports to both a functional (or divisional) manager and to a project (or group) manager.

MBA
Master of Business Administration.

Mechanistic organization
An organization in which the operations are rule-based.

Mediation
A situation in which a third party assists two parties in conflict to reach an agreement.

Mentors
Individuals who pass on the benefits of their knowledge and experience to younger and less experienced individuals.

Message
Encoded information sent by a sender to a receiver.

Meta-analysis
Statistical method for estimating the true correlation between two variables from the distribution of sample correlations corrected for the

different size of samples, restrictions in range, and its limits from the results obtained from several individual samples or studies.

Middle managers
Managers at the middle levels of the organizational hierarchy, who are responsible for the direction of the lower-level supervisors reporting to them.

Mission
The stated purposes of the organization.

Model
A facsimile that captures the important essentials of reality; may be conceptual, mathematical, or physical.

Modeling
Learning by imitation; behaving in the same way as observed in another person to make a certain response.

Moral identity
Awareness of one's own moral beliefs and ethical behaviour, and of their importance to oneself.

Morality
Set of social beliefs and values of right conduct.

Multinational corporation (MNC)
A corporation with operations and divisions in numerous countries, but that is controlled by headquarters in one country.

Multinational firm
An organization that locates, trades, or produces products or offers services in several countries.

N

Negative reinforcement
See Aversive reinforcement.

Network
A pattern of interconnections among individuals, groups, or organizations.

Nonprogrammed decisions
Specific solutions that emerge from unstructured processes to deal with nonroutine problems.

Norms
Shared group expectations about behaviour; socially defined and enforced standards about how the world should be interpreted and how one should behave in it.

O

Objectives
The targeted goals of individuals, groups, or organizations toward which resources and efforts are channeled.

Occupation
A collection of similar jobs existing in different firms.

One-way communication
Any communication from the sender without a reply from the receiver.

Operational definition
A specification of the procedures or operations by which a concept is sensed and measured.

Operations research

Mathematical techniques for modeling, analysis, and solution of management problems.

Organic organization

An organization in which operations are subject to modification through learning from feedback.

Organizational climate

Employees' attitudes toward the organization and their satisfaction with it.

Organizational conflict

Disagreement between organizational members and groups over the allocation of scarce resources, or how to engage in interdependent work activities; disagreements arising from different assumptions, goals, identifications, or statuses.

Organizational culture

The norms, values, attitudes, and beliefs, evidenced in myths, stories, jargon, and rituals that are shared by organizational members.

Organizational design

The creation of the organizational structure that is most appropriate for the strategy, people, technology, and tasks of the organization.

Organizational development

A long-range effort to improve an organization's problem-solving and renewal process.

Organizational goals

An organization's purpose, mission, and objectives that form the basis of its strategy.

Organizational structure

The arrangement and interrelationship of the various components and positions in an organization.

Organization chart
A diagram displaying the functions, departments, and positions in an organization.

Overload
The lack of capacity to meet performance expectations.

P

Partial reinforcement
A schedule of reinforcement in which rewards are given intermittently.

Path-goal analysis
The means and ways that describe what objectives can be reached.

Patriarchal
A male-dominated family or society in which the men are much more in power and control than are the women.

Perception
An immediately sensed experience of other persons or objects, modified and organized by the perceiver's personal characteristics and by social influences.

Performance appraisal
The evaluation of an individual's performance by comparing it to standards or objectives.

Peripheral routing
Persuading people unable or unmotivated to accept the idea.

Personality
The dynamic organization of the abilities, attitudes, beliefs, and motives of a particular individual that contribute to the individual's reaction to his or her environment.

Placebo

A substance or a condition used as an experimental control, which should have no effects relevant to the experiment.

Policy

General guidelines for decision making.

Population

The total collection of people or cases from which a sample is drawn.

Position power

Power that is inherent in the formal position occupied by the incumbent.

Positive reinforcer

The consequence of behaviour that is desirable, pleasant, or needed. When linked to the behaviour, the positive reinforcer increases the probability that the behaviour will be repeated in the same or similar situations.

Power structure

A set of relationships among different members or units of an organization that is based on the differences in power among them.

Prejudice

A negative evaluation of a person because of the person's sex, age, race, ethnicity, or membership in another group or organization.

Process consultation

Consultation in which members of an organization are helped to understand and change the ways in which they work together.

Productivity

Performance relative to resources; output divided by input; quantity and quality of output in a given period.

Programmed decisions
Solutions to routine problems determined by rules, procedures, or habits.

Projection
The attribution of one's own motives to others, usually unconsciously or subconsciously.

Prototype
An idealized image or the first of its kind on which copies are based.

Pseudo transformational leadership
A false messiah who appears to act like a transformational leader but is actually inauthentic and self-interested and leads the group, organization, or society astray.

Psychological contract
Mutual expectations between an individual and an organization or between subordinates and superiors of how work is to be performed and how they will relate to each other; the rights, privileges, and obligations of each to each other.

Psychosocial
Psychological elements combine with social aspects to affect relationships.

Purpose
The primary role of an organization in society in producing goods or services.

Q

Quality circles
Periodic meetings of employees and management personnel to solve quality, production, and related problems.

Quality control

The process that ensures that goods and services meet predetermined standards.

Quality of work life

The value of work that takes into account the well-being of the employee as well as that of the organization.

R

R & D

Research and development.

Rational approach

An approach in which conclusions are arrived at by reasoning.

Rational-economic man

A theory that fully informed people are motivated primarily by money and self-interest.

Rationally-oriented leadership

Relies on logical and methodical reasoning.

Recency effect

The predominant effect of the most recent information received on learning, retention, judgment, or opinion about persons, objects, or issues.

Reference group

A group with whom a person identifies and compares him or herself.

Reinforcement

The consequence of behaviour that influences whether the behaviour will be evoked again under the same or similar stimulus conditions.

Reinforcement schedule
The pattern of reinforcement that can affect how quickly behaviour is modified, shaped, and learned, and how resistant it is to change or extinction.

Relative deprivation
The tendency to be dissatisfied with one's own status and compensation relative to that of those with whom one compares oneself, to expectations, and to comparable conditions.

Reliability
The consistency of measurement, as seen in the stability of scores over time or in the equivalence of scores on two forms of a test of the same attributes (see Coefficient alpha).

Reputational capital
Intangible corporate value enhanced by executive leadership, quality of products, publicized awards, and rankings.

Resilience
Ability to deal with adversity.

Risk ratio
Maximum risk compared with probability of success.

Risky shift
The tendency for groups to make a decision that is less conservative than one that would be made alone by each of its individual members.

Role
A socially defined pattern of behaviour that is expected of an individual in a designated function in a particular position within a group, organization, or society.

Role conflict

A situation in which persons are faced with meeting conflicting demands. Conflict can arise between values within a role, between competing roles, or from the demands of others.

Role overload

A situation in which role requirements exceed the limits of time, resources, and capabilities.

S

Sample

A portion of a population that is selected for study in lieu of the complete population.

Scapegoating

The displacement of hostility toward a weaker available target when the source of frustration is too powerful or not available for attack.

Scientific method

The systematic use of deduction, induction, and verification of predictions by the collection of relevant data.

Self-actualization

Using one's capacities fully in meaningful, personally satisfying endeavours.

Self-concept

The way people perceive and evaluate themselves.

Self-fulfilling prophecy

The expectation of a reality influences the fulfillment of that reality.

Social distance

The acceptable degree of closeness (physical, social, or psychological) between leaders and subordinates and between members of particular ethnic groups.

Socialization

Learning the norms of one's group, organization, or society and acquiring its distinctive values, beliefs, and characteristics.

Social loafing

A condition in which workers reduce or withhold effort on a group task.

Specialization

The performance of only some specific part of a whole collection of tasks by an individual worker.

Staff

Individuals or groups who provide line personnel with advice and services.

Stakeholders

Individuals and groups who gain from the organization's successes and lose from its failures.

Stereotype

A standard image applied to all members of the same group that ignores the variations among them.

Strategic planning

The formulation of an organization's objectives and how to achieve them.

Structure

A pattern of prescribed or observed consistencies in relations among members of a group or organization.

Sunk costs

Money spent or resources already used.

Superego
The part of the personality that is oriented toward doing what is regarded as morally right and proper: one's conscience, ego ideal, and ideal self-image.

T

Task force
A temporary group established to address a specific problem (also Ad hoc group).

Tautology
Circular reasoning; for example, arguing that A caused B because B caused A.

Team building
Improving relationships among members and the accomplishment of the task by diagnosing problems in team processes affecting the team's performance.

Theory
A system of concepts, rules about the interconnections of the concepts, and ways of linking the concepts to observed facts.

Theory X
A theory that assumes that the average worker dislikes work, is lazy, has little ambition, and must be directed or threatened with punishment to perform adequately.

Theory Y
A theory that assumes the average worker can enjoy work and be committed, involved, and responsible.

Transformational leadership
The leader elevates the follower morally about what is important, valued, and goes beyond the simpler transactional relationship of providing reward or avoidance of punishment for compliance.

U

Unfreezing
Making old ways unacceptable so that changes are readily accepted and can occur.

V

Values
What people consider right, good, and important.

Variable
Any quantity that may take on several points on a dimension; anything that changes.

Verification
The collection of facts to support or refute hypotheses.

Vertical communication
Communication up or down the chain of command.

Visionary Leadership
Planning and forming policy that is farsighted and future-oriented, and provides direction for future actions.

W

Walk-around management
Top managers visit with employees at their workplace.

Whistle blower

Employee who voluntarily reports infractions of the rules, violations of ethics, or illegal actions by other members of the organization.

www.ingramcontent.com/pod-product-compliance
Lightning Source LLC
Chambersburg PA
CBHW040855210326
41597CB00029B/4858